HURRAH FOR HASTINGS!

A Celebration

by
Leonard Scrivens
(1911 - 1992)

Introduction and Jonnick Generations - Jottings - Parts 1 and 2
Written and compiled by
Cynthia Wright (née Scrivens)

("Jonnick" - an old Sussex expression meaning "straightforward" or "staunch")

*Dedicated to the memory of all those who have contributed
towards the colourful, unique history of Hastings and St. Leonards*

First published in 2009 by S.B. Publications
14 Bishopstone Road, Seaford, East Sussex BN25 2UB
Tel: 01323 893498 Email: sbpublications@tiscali.co.uk
www.sbpublications.co.uk

ISBN 978-185770-3498

Designed and Typeset by EH Graphics, East Sussex (01273) 515527

❦ Contents ❦

Outside Front Cover: Photograph by Arthur Moulton, showing 58 All Saints Street, Old Town, Hastings, 1880s. D. Gibbs, Coal Merchant, advertises: *Best House, Second House, Kitchen, Best Nuts, Kitchen Nuts. Coke at Gas Price. Furniture Removed on Moderate Terms. Orders Received.* To the right are the initials H.C.I.S. of the Hastings Cottage Improvement Society, which was founded in 1857 and incorporated in 1861.

Outside Back Cover: Two Judge postcards. *Extraordinary High Tide at Hastings, 26th November, 1905.* Possibly earliest postcards of local street scenes photographed at night, Fred Judge being a proponent of night-time photography. On the reverse of the "boat" card, Alice Morris (later Scrivens) asks her future sister-in-law, "How would you like to row round the Memorial instead of <u>tramming</u> it?", a reference to the newly-introduced tramway system. The clearly visible *Albert Memorial Clock* shows 11:15 p.m., whereas the detail on the "central figure" card tells us the image was taken five minutes earlier, at 11:10 p.m. *The Memorial* was demolished in 1973.

All royalties from sales will go to the Old Hastings Preservation Society, Registered Charity No. 221623.
Additionally, the compiler is buying from the publishers, S.B. Publications,
100 copies of the book and giving these to the O.H.P.S. for the Society to sell.
The Old Hastings Preservation Society is based at: Hastings History House, 21 Courthouse Street, Hastings, East Sussex TN34 3AU
Tel: (01424) 424744   Email: ohps@ohps.org.uk   www.ohps.org.uk

Acknowledgements

First and foremost, *HURRAH FOR HASTINGS!* would never have seen the light of day had it not been for the enthusiastic reception afforded it by the ever-busy and dedicated Vice-Chairman of the Old Hastings Preservation Society, Dennis Collins, to whom I express my gratitude. I also wish to thank Victoria Williams, former Curator of Hastings Museums & Art Gallery, who, very many years ago, kindly read my original top-heavy manuscript, then covering the whole of East Sussex, and was encouraging.

I have very much appreciated the unfailing help and information provided by members of staff at Hastings Reference Library, in alphabetical order:- Roger Bristow, Gillian Newman, Paul McNicol, Shelley Morrow, Thea Allan Torriset.

I also wish to thank Elizabeth Howe of E H Graphics for her skill regarding the reproduction of the illustrative material (sometimes awkward) and her knowledge and advice concerning the lay-out of the book. I am grateful also to Lindsay Woods of S.B. Publications who, amongst other things, introduced me to Elizabeth Howe, and to Chris Howden who gave general advice.

As will be noticed, the work of many photographers (including that of Francis Frith) is featured within the following pages. Some material remains, to this day, anonymous. We owe them all a great debt of gratitude as they have provided us with fascinating and informative glimpses of long-vanished Hastings and St. Leonards. There are too many photographers to list here individually and so, although it is probably invidious to single out any one in particular, special mention <u>must</u> be made of Fred Judge (whose name is recognised the world over) and of whom my father wrote briefly, in 1978/79: "Judge, a Yorkshireman, came to Hastings with a brother in 1902. He took over an existing business at 21a Wellington Place, subsequently moving to White Rock and then to Havelock Road with a retail shop in Robertson Street (the famous Judge's Corner). Outlets were established in London and the Provinces, and following closure at Robertson Street, a shop was opened at Marine Court, St. Leonards. These retail premises were all closed eventually, but the business still continues at Bulverhythe. The most famous image of Hastings ever printed, *Glory*, was taken by Fred Judge in October 1906. This was reproduced in almost every size, earned numerous awards and, as a postcard, sold many hundreds of thousands. Judge died in 1950." Happily, in 2009 the business still flourishes in Bexhill Road, St. Leonards.

There are references to numerous authors and their writings, and some of the many Guides issued, the first published in 1794. (See particularly my Appendix). Brief mention must be made of John Manwaring Baines (one of the founders of the Old Hastings Preservation Society) and two of his books, the renowned "Historic Hastings" (1955) and "Burton's St. Leonards" (1956). In addition to his active involvement with local historical groups, the then Curator of Hastings Museums & Art Gallery was a scholarly and entertaining writer, publishing books on subjects as diverse as Sussex Pottery and Hastings Grammar School, the latter being co-written with L.R. Conisbee. A Yorkshireman (like Fred Judge), he also contributed to the long defunct (and excellent) Sussex County Magazine which ran from December 1926 to July 1956, and wrote informative Museum booklets from the 1930s onwards.

Finally, I thank my husband, John, whose ideas, suggestions and support have been invaluable.

Cynthia Wright (née Scrivens) 2009

THE EAST SUSSEX HOSPITAL CAKE – 2ND JULY, 1912

East Sussex Hospital Cake. July 2nd./12.

This postcard is referred to on Page 73 - local fishing boats are featured on the cake, as well as summer activities (such as cricket, cycling, croquet), fruits and roses. At the base (presumably crafted in sugar) is a representation of Sir Luke Fildes's painting "The Doctor", from 1891 - a highly appropriate choice! According to Christopher Wood's book "Victorian Painting", this was one of the most popular of all Victorian paintings. He states that over a million engravings of it were sold and for years it was a favourite at the Tate Gallery. Again per Wood - in his search for authenticity Fildes had a complete replica of the interior of a fisherman's cottage built in his studio. Addison's (long established and much missed) were based at Marina, St. Leonards, and are discussed on Page 73.

—∘ Preface ∘—

HURRAH FOR HASTINGS! has been simmering on the back-burner in various guises for ten years. My one regret is that I have been forced to omit so much - a quart does not fit into a pint pot! Excluding my own memories, the "cut-off" point has been, with a few exceptions, the First World War. The book is intended as a celebration of the town, not a history of the Scrivens family, although there are references, particularly with regard to the *Hastings Old Bank*.

Briefly, in 1779 William Scrivens became landlord of the illustrious High Street *Swan* coaching inn. William, with his son and two grandsons, had a considerable impact on the development of Hastings & St. Leonards. Aside from Civic/Mayoral responsibilities, innkeeping, library, banking and legal concerns, they were much involved with social issues such as housing within the Old Town - hence Scrivens Buildings, erected 1872/73, part of the Hastings Cottage Improvement Society, of which one Scrivens was a founder. The Buildings' site in Crown Lane is now occupied by Crown Court, and the significance of the original development is outlined within the book. There were active ties to associations such as the Literary Institution, Mechanics Institution, Hastings Working Men's Club and the Y.M.C.A. Following formation of the Hastings Grammar School Foundation in 1878, the newly-built school opened in Nelson Road in 1883. It had been hoped that George Scrivens, the last surviving trustee of Parker's Charity, would lay the foundation stone on 6th September 1882, but illness prevented this. Family members were closely linked with the Hastings & St. Leonards Gas Co., two being proprietors and directors from its establishment in 1832, George maintaining his link from that year until death in 1887, having been Chairman from 1873. As Mayor, William Scrivens welcomed Princess Victoria at the time of her visit in 1834: his son (also William), Chairman of the Hastings Pier Company, died in 1871 during his Mayoral term, so failing to witness the grand official opening of the Pier in 1872. The deaths of brothers William and George, each childless, meant that this branch of the family died out.

The book is unconventional and quirky in format: there is no Index as one would have been superfluous. Some may consider the section relating to half a century ago too recent to be included, but I feel that memories from *all* eras should be valued equally: life in the 1950s and 1960s was vastly different from that of today. Towns everywhere have always experienced change, but this nowadays occurs faster than ever and, as a result, so much is easily forgotten or lost. I am reminded of a particular afternoon in St. Leonards during the 1960s. Knowing of my father's interest in local history, Dr. William Hoadley Gabb (of the much respected Gabb medical family) unexpectedly showed him, and discussed *at leisure*, maternity records from the town dating back many generations. The pace of life was certainly less frenetic then.

I hope this book will have a broad appeal, particularly amongst newcomers and visitors to the town. Perhaps even the scholarly will discover something, unknown previously, within my father's writings. Above all, please enjoy *HURRAH FOR HASTINGS!* and remember that, when you buy a copy, you are helping the Old Hastings Preservation Society, the financial benefits to which are detailed within my Introduction.

—◄∘►—

THE HASTINGS ALPHABET.

A's Andrew's Archway, so ugly and narrow,
  Why you scarcely have hand-room for trundling a barrow.

B are the 'Busses that make your limbs quiver,
  But the Doctors all say—that is "good for the liver."

C stands for the County Conservative Club,
  I expect now and then they've a rub-a-dub-dub.

D are the Drink Shops that sadly abound,
  I *should* like to level them all to the ground.

E the Electric Lights, blinking and winking,
  There's room for improvement, to my way of thinking.

F is the Fish Market, would it were down,
  For it's not ornamental at all to the Town.

G will stand very well for the Good Templar Lodges,
  Let the members beware of the many drink dodges.

H is the Harbour, that is, when completed,
  But for lack of the needful, the work is defeated.

I are the Institutes, equalled by none,
  Where much good is, at any rate, *meant* to be done.

J Jumble Sales—such a capital plan
  To get rid of your rubbish as quick as you can.

K the kind feeling pervading the Town
  When Members of Royalty *cannot* come down.

L is the Lift, that will save you the walking,
  Whereby you'll have all the more breath for the talking.

M's the Memorial, by night and day,
  A capital land mark, that's *all* I can say.

N is the Noise that so often is made
  About all the noises along the Parade.

O's the "Observer," so brimful o' news,
  That *that* is the Paper the *wise* people choose.

P's the Parade, and a splendid one too,
  Notwithstanding there's been such a hallabulloo.

Q is the "Queen's," that most regal Hotel,
  But remember the "Grand" and the "Palace" as well.

R are the Rates and the Taxes so heavy,
  I vote we protest against them in a bevy.

S are the Steamers that take you to France,
  And sometimes they lead you a bit of a dance.

T Total Abstainers, I wish there were more,
  Tho' sometimes considered a terrible bore.

U is the Union, down in a hole,
  Do the inmates complain of the Ratepayers' dole?

V are the Visitors—welcome enough,
  Don't drive them away by the Trams and such stuff.

W it must stand for the Warrior Square,
  If you want to make use of their Gardens, Beware!

X are the 'Xcellent strains of the Band,
  Don't you think they deserve a more elegant Stand?

Y the Young People in Robertson Street,
  Who think it so lovely each other to meet.

Z is the *Zeal* the Town Councillors show
  In promoting the *good of the Town*, don't you know!

                    F.M.L.

Budd & Gillatt, Printers, South Street, St. Leonards.

Author and date of *The Hastings Alphabet* unknown, but must be post-1905 as trams are mentioned. However, *Andrew's Archway* features, so perhaps poetic licence has been employed! (See Page 45 re: *St. Andrew's Arch*).

No. *122*   CERTIFICATE.

Ann Honeysett aged *1½*, was Vaccinated the *10 June* 184*7*, by me, and passed re v and successfully through the Disease.

(Signed,) *Frede Wallis*
Surgn

You are desired to attend next _____ that the Certificate may be filled up.*

*The above Certificate in blank, should be given to the Person on whom the operation of Vaccination has been performed, or to the Parent, Nurse, or other Person having the care of the Child, immediately after the operation.

FAMILY PICTURES

Above left: Vaccination certificate for Ann Honeysett (Hunnisett), later Morris, from 1847. See Page 20 for detail on Surgeon Wallis of Bexhill.

Below left: Henry and Ann Morris photographed in the very early 1900s at the *U.S.A. Studios*, 1, 3 & 5 Palace Avenue, White Rock, Hastings. Henry's sister, Mary, married George H. Brett, well-known Baldslow monumental mason, Parish Clerk of Hollington Church-in-the-Wood, and Hollington Bailiff to Sir Archibald Lamb of *Beauport*.

Right: Alice Morris, youngest child of Henry and Ann, married Thomas Scrivens in 1910 at St. Matthew's Church, Silverhill, St. Leonards. The photograph of Alice was taken in 1907 and that of Tom in 1906. Neither photographer known. (See Page 17).

Left: Alice Morris, aged five, (youngest Morris child) with her slightly older brother, Bertie, photographed by J.Birchall, *The Cambridge Studio*, Cambridge Road, Hastings, on 5th November 1889. At that time there were many photographic studios and the family seemed to favour a great number of them. Some work, such as that from W.A.Thomas, 45a George Street, Old Town, is still within original glassine wrappers, thereby protecting the images. The stout boots worn by Alice were made for her by her father. In 1908 Bertie emigrated to New Zealand by *RMS Ionic*, married, and eventually returned on two separate occasions, by boat, with his family to visit relations.

Centre: Henry and Ann Morris had nine children but, sadly, Caroline Matilda died from tubercular meningitis in 1881, aged nine. As a local social history "insight", the report of the funeral service, and subsequent proceedings involving Carrie's schoolfriends, is reproduced, this piece appearing in the *Hastings & St. Leonards Observer* of 14th May 1881.

Right: Annie/Nance (Mary Ann) Morris, eldest Morris child, (1868 - 1956), pictured by F.S. Mann, Wellington Place, Hastings, 1885. (Photograph is "spotted" due to age). Annie had to give up teaching due to poor health and never married. Alice, born in 1884, died in 1969. *(See Jonnick Generations - Jottings - Parts 1 and 2)*. There was enormous social change during each sister's lifetime.

and 30 guineas, and, with very few exceptions, all were sold.

CHURCH OF ENGLAND BAND OF HOPE SOCIETY.— The remains of Caroline Matilda Morris, one of the members of the Silverdale Branch of the above Society, were interred in the Hastings Cemetery on Saturday last. Several of the Band of Hope children, wearing their badges, followed in procession, also some of the teachers and scholars from St. Matthew's Day and Sunday Schools, with which she was connected. The service having been impressively read by the Chaplain, a special hymn, composed for the occasion by the missionary of Silverdale, was sung by the children, also the well-known and appropriate lines, "My God, my Father, while I stray," &c. Several wreaths and flowers, prepared by willing hands and loving hearts, were strewn upon the coffin. On the following afternoon, the Rev. C. Rolfe addressed the children attending St. Matthew's Sunday School in a most impressive manner, on the subject of "Death." Hymns were sung by the children appropriate for the occasion. On the evening following, a special sermon was preached by the missionary of Silverdale, from the words, "The Master is come, and calleth for thee." John xi. 28.

NEW COMERS.—As the town progresses we have fresh tradesmen coming among us and

SILVERHILL, ST. LEONARDS

Above: Fascia board for **E. Howell, Stationer,** publisher of all four cards here.

Below: Bird's-eye view of Silverhill at turn of 20th century.

Above: St. Matthew's Church, Silverhill.

Below: Silverhill Junction, tram, and milk churns (?from Catt of Alma Terrace? as address on handcart). Posted 1906. In 1911, E.G. Catt advertised "The Silverhill Dairy". (See 1911 Silverhill Year Book and Souvenir).

HUNNISETT FAMILY PICTURES

c. 1880s / 1890s
(the name is sometimes spelled "Honeysett")

Left: John Thomas Hunnisett/Honeysett (born 1848), known as "Jack", and wife, Sarah, with some of their children in a boat on the Bexhill shingle. Photographer unknown.

Centre: Jack Hunnisett here photographed by R.B.Hutchinson, 52 Robertson Street, Hastings, in formal pose, wearing thigh-length waders necessary for his beach work. (See L.J.Bartley's *The Story of Bexhill*, 1971, Page 102, for full details of the well-known Hunnisett Bexhill bathing and boating station). Noted local artist Charles Graves featured personalised Hunnisett bathing-machines within his beach views.
See also *Jonnick Generations - Jottings - Part 1*, Page 20.

Right: Jack Hunnisett outside his "hut" on Bexhill beach, ready for hard work. Note lifebelt and personalised sweater. Jack's obituary notice described him as a "hard-working man much given to minding his own business and leaving other people alone". Photographer unknown.

BOREHAM STREET POST OFFICE & VILLAGE STORES, NEAR HERSTMONCEUX

c. 1884

Now *Scolfe's Tearooms* and listed Grade II, dating from the 1300s. Photographer unknown.

Although outside the area covered by the book, Boreham Street is mentioned within the text due to strong family links through marriage. Harriet Eliza Morris, an older sister of Alice Morris (later Scrivens) married George Austin (1882-1956) who is pictured here as a babe-in-arms. Nathan Austin, his father, (at extreme left) had a thriving business as described within *Jonnick Generations - Jottings - Part 2*, and was highly astute, with other local interests, too. George followed his father into the family business. After marriage, Harriet (always known as "Hart") had responsibility for running the Post Office. Mr. Trigger (at extreme right) was perhaps bored with the length of time then involved when a photograph was taken and obviously moved at the vital moment! A brief outline of the building's very colourful, interesting history is given towards the end of *Jonnick Generations - Jottings - Part 2*, and later postcards appear, giving an impression of the size of the premises, along with a photograph of young Harriet from 1891. (See Pages 13, 77 and 78).

BOREHAM STREET POST OFFICE & VILLAGE STORES
very early 1900s and c. 1930

Left: Harriet Eliza Morris pictured by W. E. A. Drinkwater, photographer, 31 Havelock Road, Hastings, 19th October 1891, occasion unknown, when she was aged seventeen. (Harriet was the older sister who accompanied Alice and their father on the upper deck of the first tram to run in Hastings for the general public in 1905). Until their deaths, George Austin and Harriet (his wife) lived alongside the Stores in an attached (but separate) property - not visible here - known then as *The Nook* (recently *Japonica Cottage*) also historically of interest being listed Grade II and dating from the 1700s, and deceptively roomy. (The compiler recalls the stone-flagging in the kitchen, a wealth of oak timbering, and the disused well in the back garden). Harriet died in 1950 and George in 1956, he having been one of the first to be treated for diabetes with insulin at the Royal East Sussex Hospital, Hastings, in the 1920s.

Below left: Very early 1900s advertising postcard. Note motor-car (uncommon sight then) parked outside Stores. There was plenty of stabling (not visible here) for horse-drawn transport. Before marriage, and during the bicycling "craze", George Austin thought nothing of cycling from Boreham Street to Silverhill and back in one day, having visited Harriet at home in St. Leonards. (Page 21 has detail on a memorable carrier's cart journey from St. Leonards to Boreham Street).

Below right: c. 1930. Note advertisements for *Mazawattee Tea*, *Nestle's Milk*, and *Colman's Starch*. Slightly more motor transport visible in the area. Three telegraph poles now apparent. *The Bull's Head Hotel* appears on right. (See Pages 12, 77 and 78).

THE LIFEBOAT MEN

Author and date unknown

When you lie in your bed on a winter's night
And you wake to the sound of the raging storm
And the windows creak and the curtains blow
And you know that the only place that's warm
In the whole wide world is the bed you're in
And you pull the blankets up to your chin
There's a ship off-shore on the storm-tossed deep
And she's trying to ride out a force-ten gale
But the wind's too strong and the sea's too steep
And the anchor drags and the engines fail
As the ice-tipped waves break over the deck
- And the rocks stand by to break up the wreck.

But there's other men lying in bed ashore
And in beds as warm and as cosy as yours
When the warning sounds at the hour of four
And they up and they dress and they run out-of-doors
Down the empty street to the snow-clad quay
Where they launch the lifeboat and put to sea
And they round the headland and battle their way
Through the mountainous waves and the blinding spray

And the lifeboat shudders and heaves and groans
As she turns their stomachs and rattles their bones
While they look for a sign in the hell ahead
- And the rocks prepare to receive their dead.

And they wallow and skid through the raging seas
In the teeth of the gale and the driving snow
As they fight for balance on flexing knees
And the dread of disaster begins to grow
- Though with never a thought for their own welfare
When the look-out suddenly spots a flare
And a cheer goes up as their hopes renew
And the boat draws near to the stricken ship
And with matchless courage they winch the crew
As they lurch and shudder and slide and slip
Then they sail for home with their salvaged mates
- As the dawn comes up and the wind abates.

And so, as you awake from your restful sleep
And you walk to the window and look outside
At a day which has snatched more lives from the deep
For the lifeboat men you will feel great pride
In the wonderful selfless work they do
For the likes of me and the likes of you.

Although *not* relating specifically to Hastings (see reference to "quay" for instance), the poem is included here as its content is particularly atmospheric.

(The first Hastings lifeboat was built in the mid-1830s, and the RNLI took control in 1858).

LAUNCH OF THE HASTINGS LIFEBOAT. APRIL 25 1908
NO 5.   SHOWING HEAVILY   6.40 P.M.   PHOTO BY JUDGES

Left: The launch of the lifeboat, Charles Arkcoll II from Bopeep, St. Leonards, on 25th April 1908 during atrocious blizzard conditions. All the crew of the London sailing barge Amy were saved, and the barge was rescued, too. Judge postcard.

⸻ ❧ Introduction ❧ ⸻

I am so pleased that the Old Hastings Preservation Society (O. H. P. S.) has given its seal of approval to *Hurrah for Hastings!*, this being a celebration of the premier Cinque Port's unique and characterful past before the advent of 20th century planners. At the very end of the Society's Newsletter for September 2007, Anne Scott, Chairman, writes, "History matters". How true! In a nutshell, the study of the past helps us, in many ways, to understand the present day. History has shaped us all.

The purpose behind the publication of this book is to raise funds for the O. H. P. S., founded in 1952, and recently established at its permanent base, *The History House*, 21 Courthouse Street, in the Old Town. All royalties from sales will go to the O. H. P. S. and, additionally, I am buying from the Publishers, S. B. Publications, 100 copies of the book and giving these to the O. H. P. S. for the Society to sell.

Briefly, the Society aims to encourage an interest in, and appreciation of, the history of the entire Borough of Hastings & St. Leonards. This is achieved in different ways, perhaps the most obvious being the championing of the town's rich fishing heritage and proud lifeboat tradition within the renowned and extended *Fishermen's Museum* (originally Church) in Rock-a-Nore Road, the running of which is the responsibility of the O. H. P. S. In addition to permanent displays (which are continually being added to), temporary exhibitions are mounted. Entry is free, but donations are welcomed. For very many centuries the fishing industry has been at the heart of the local community and Hastings is well-known for its beach-based fleet. Officially recognised as an environmentally friendly fishery, it has *Marine Stewardship Council* certificates covering Dover Sole, Herring and Mackerel. The *Hastings Fish Community Interest Company* was set up by local fishermen to retain, for the good of their community, more of the profits from selling fish landed in Hastings.

The History House hosts displays on all facets of local history, as well as holding a wide range of topical / associated publications available for sale. Talks on a variety of subjects are held and guided walks are enjoyed, too. A special effort is made in the summer at the time of *Old Town Carnival Week*, as well as, in the autumn, during *Hastings Week*, this always incorporating 14th October which commemorates *The Battle of Hastings* in 1066 - undoubtedly the most significant date in English history, it being the last time we were defeated on home soil. Hastingers have always known how to enjoy themselves, this characteristic evidenced, for example, by the celebrations staged in the Old Town to coincide with the Coronation, on 28th June 1838, of Queen Victoria. The crowning of the "Queen of All Saints" (Anne Page) took place outside 117 (later 134) All Saints Street with many prominent local figures taking part, including William Lucas Shadwell and Frederick North. After the ceremony, when "Her Majesty" had removed her "Coronation Robes", tea was taken in the street to the strains of *Polly put the kettle on* and, in the evening, a dance was held on the high pavement. Anne, a well-known local character and the widow of George Page (a riding officer at Hastings), died aged 81 in 1849. Such exuberance continues today, with the O. H. P. S. at the forefront of celebrations which, in addition to the fun, raise funds for various good causes, including the Society itself.

Not to be overlooked is the highly important role played by the Society in keeping a close eye on local planning issues and although this is, sadly, often a thankless task and reminiscent of King Canute's attempt to control the waves, nevertheless its efforts are to be applauded and should be encouraged. New members are always welcome!

I do hope you will enjoy *Hurrah for Hastings!* which attempts to show the town, as it was, from the 1850s to the early 20th century, and during the 1950s/1960s. Perhaps you will learn something of which you were unaware and be encouraged to delve deeper into the fascinating history of Hastings & St. Leonards. But, first of all, I must explain the background to this publication - a tale in its own right.

⸻ ◇ ⸻

THE FIRST WORLD WAR - CAPTURED IN FRANCE - 21st MARCH 1918

Dear Mrs. Scrivens,

I much regret to inform you that your husband became "missing" on the 21st of last month. The Company were in the line on that date and your husband was at Company Headquarters in the line, though usually he has not gone into the line with the Company on previous occasions. I was not there myself but the officers who were there say that the headquarters were surrounded early in the day and after fighting with rifles gallantly for several hours, retired along a trench and mostly escaped; one man was actually captured and got away again in safety. Unfortunately your husband, exhausted by the fighting and running, could not keep up with the others and when last seen was unwounded, it is almost certain that he would be captured a few minutes later, and the Boche was treating his prisoners well that day. Having been with the Company since its formation, he is much missed; acting as Mess Cook, he was indefatigable and no trouble seemed too much for him, whether it was getting a meal ready for an officer coming in at 2am from the line or setting off at 5 o'clock in the morning, or anything else. With every hope and confidence that he will return alive and well after the war is over and that you will hear from him before long,

I am, yours sincerely,
H.K. Boyle Capt

"D" Coy 30th M. G. Battn
8/4/18

Letter (referred to within text) written by Captain H.K. Boyle, D Company, 30th Machine Gun Battalion, to Alice Scrivens (née Morris) on 8th April 1918, following the capture of Thomas Scrivens on 21st March 1918 during the First War. The letter was received by Alice in Silverhill on 12th April 1918. Original letter within envelope, and contents reproduced here.

See Page 22 for detail from Tom's first letter home dated 4th April 1918.

The photograph of Thomas Scrivens (1884 - 1942) on left was taken by H. Seymour Cousens (St. Leonards-on-Sea) on 14th May 1917.

Jonnick Generations = Jottings = Part 1

The subject matter is primarily a selection of photographs (copies of some being taken in 1978 by various interested parties) and notes from the collection of my late father, Leonard Scrivens (1911-1992), known as Len within the family, and a member of the O. H. P. S. until his death. Modest, unassuming and very independently-minded, with a deep love of the town, sadly he was forced through ill-health to leave Hastings in 1980. He would have been highly delighted to know that his material is now, for the benefit of the O. H. P. S., being put to such good use. I hope he would not have objected too strongly to my having edited his writings, some of which, with the passage of thirty years, are not relevant here. From early boyhood he read widely, being particularly interested in material relating to Hastings and, over time, he amassed a sizeable collection, becoming, in his quiet way, very knowledgeable about the area which meant so much to him.

A great deal of confusion is caused due to the popularity, within the Scrivens family, of the first name "William", this being the name of three of four members from three successive generations of one branch commemorated in the plaque in Crown Lane, Old Town. The confusion is further compounded as my father's side of the family favoured the name, too. When William Scrivens (one of the four proprietors of the first circulating library, initially in Croft Road) arrived in the town from Dorking in 1779, aged 39, to become innkeeper of the renowned (and long-gone) coaching inn, *The Swan*, now the site of a garden of remembrance in the High Street, my father's paternal forebears were innkeepers too, in Portsmouth. On *The Hard*, (with its Dickensian *Nicholas Nickleby* associations) they were in business for generations, and Nelson might well have been familiar with their inn. The Portsmouth establishment was very rumbustious and rowdy, not at all like the decorous *Swan*, with its fine Assembly Room, tea-drinkings every Sunday evening, and where there was never any trouble. Mentioned in 1523, *The Swan* was particularly popular during the 18th and 19th centuries. Rebuilt in 1879, it was finally destroyed by enemy action in 1943.

Len's grandfather, William Scrivens, left Portsmouth, probably in the 1860s, travelling on foot to Dorking, where he eventually set up home on the outskirts, in North Holmwood. In those days, walking long distances was very much an accepted part of everyday life and was not considered at all unusual. The only other methods of travelling inland were by the railway system (still, relatively speaking, in its infancy), by some form of horse-drawn transport, or on horseback. In due course his family became well-known in the area, particularly his eldest son, inevitably named William. Clerk to the Board of Guardians, he had responsibility for the 1911 Dorking census, and was also Registrar for Births, Marriages and Deaths. Another son, Alfred, became Master of Hillingdon Workhouse, now Hillingdon Hospital. (Not all Workhouse Masters were draconian, as is popularly supposed). Alfred's wife, Edith, supported her husband as Matron. Thomas Scrivens, Len's father, was the youngest child, born in 1884, his mother dying soon after his birth, and he was brought up by an older sister. Following childhood illness, regular, recuperative morning walks were taken on Southsea Common, near Portsmouth, in the company of a relation always referred to as "Mrs. Colonel Popham". Afterwards, both adult <u>and youngster</u> were fortified by a glass of Madeira wine and a slice of sponge cake.

In 1910, Tom married Alice Morris (also born in 1884) at *St. Matthew's Church*, Silverhill. Alice was the youngest child of Henry and Ann Morris of Silverhill, the two families already known to each other by way of a Morris marriage connection with the Thanet branch of the Scrivens family. Described on his marriage certificate as "Fishmonger", Tom was noted widely for his culinary skills - perhaps a throw-back to the innkeeping days in Portsmouth? Alice's cousins, Rosie and Polly Marchant, were bridesmaids. (See Page 8).

The Morris family by that stage was running a well-established boot and shoemaking business known as *Silverhill Boot Stores*, which was based at 64 Sedlescombe Road North, then a very rural area (difficult to believe now). The *Stores* catered for all types of boots and shoes and Len's maternal grandfather, Henry Morris, (who remembered Alexandra Park as a hop-garden and farmland) and uncle (Harry Morris) mastered an old skill involving the complexities of handling different types of leather needed for a variety of footwear. Great manual dexterity was required, too, plus knowledge of the specialist tools involved. Henry Morris had originally started out in life as a stonemason - probably due to the fact that, in the early 1800s, his father had had a brickyard and quarry at the top of Red Lane, now Harrow Lane and built over. Unfortunately, one day when at work on *Christ Church*, in London Road, St. Leonards, Henry fell, severely damaging his foot. Unable to continue as a stonemason, he turned instead to boot and shoemaking. I have no idea where he learned his trade, a skill which would have taken considerable time to perfect.

Tough, everyday working boots were made, as well as different kinds of shoes for women and children. Len remembered having shoes made for him, when a small boy, by his grandfather. A regular visitor, well-known to the Morris family, was Charles Graves, the noted artist, who lived nearby, and special fishing boots were required by Charles Ebden, barrister, of *Baldslow Place*, when on his estate in Scotland. The architect Norman Shaw had been responsible for the design of *Baldslow Place* (now *Claremont School*) and it was built in 1878/79 for Mr. Ebden at a cost of approximately £9,000. Particular care had to be taken when delivering shoes to the home of Captain and Mrs. Woodruffe at *Old Roar House*, Silverhill, as fierce arguments were often raging between them - on one noteworthy occasion a bowl of rice pudding came flying through an open window, having been thrown by a furious Mrs. Woodruffe. The *Stores* employed a young lad who was completely deaf and Alice, Len's mother, learned to be skilled at sign-language as a result. When *Russell & Bromley* were established in London Road, St. Leonards, in 1907, certain shoes were supplied, and all repair work was done, by *Silverhill Boot Stores*. How the family laughed at people remarking that they would never go anywhere but *Russell & Bromley!* I still use, around the home today, a very long, sturdy pair of brass and wood clippers, dating from about 1920, originally used for retrieving shoes from the front of the shop window. (Plate 6, Page 103, shows an example of Charles Graves's work).

Alice was a feisty girl, with an enquiring mind, who had been what was known in Victorian times as a "pupil-teacher" at *St. Matthew's Day School* in Silverhill and she would dearly have loved to become a full-blown teacher in time. However, her parents forbade this, as Annie (their eldest daughter) had tried her hand at teaching locally but (never strong) had been forced to give up. So, Alice remained at home. In addition to her memories of town flooding, such as on 26th November 1905, she, like all her siblings, recalled enjoying ice-skating. In a 1952 letter, Annie (born 1868) remembered the extreme cold of December 1879 when she was eleven years old. "There was skating on the reservoirs" (a reference to the newly laid-out *Alexandra Park* of 1878, later formally opened in 1882 by the Prince and Princess of Wales), "for about six weeks and the crowds there were there. I was amongst them of course". She then referred to her task of dressing the Tree on Christmas Eve: "Never before, as there was no place to keep it out of sight with all our crowd". This involved naked, lighted candles (the usual, highly dangerous practice then) and, in celebration of the special occasion, goose was always served. On the subject of food, Alice's mother was insistent upon cheese appearing on the table at every meal, including breakfast, and the family well remembered the introduction into this country, in the 1890s, of the banana, this novelty being quite a talking point everywhere, Hastings and St. Leonards included. Recovering from illness, one of the four Morris sisters expressed a strong desire to try one as she had heard so much about them. Her wish was granted, but she did not realise that the banana had to be peeled: consequently the invalid attempted to eat the whole fruit including the skin, pronouncing in no uncertain terms that it was most unappetizing! (See Page 9).

Len's mother was a keen cyclist, like her brothers, (particularly Harry, a member of the *St. Leonards Cycling Club*), always maintaining that the two inventions which had had the most impact on members of her family were the bicycle and the sewing-machine. The first made local travel much easier, and the second speeded up previously time-consuming tasks. She took a great deal of interest in local affairs and embraced the postcard "craze" of the early 1900s with much enthusiasm, there being intense, friendly rivalry regarding individual postcard collections. I have many of these cards, including some written by Alice's mother who favoured the "long s" in correspondence. As already touched on, winters certainly appeared to be more severe in the past, the seasons now being not so clearly defined. Cards of the early 1900s show heavy falls of snow within the neighbourhood and Alice, writing on 22nd November 1904 asks, "How do you like this cold weather? We shall be able to go skating soon. Our bedroom windows were frozen this morning". This was not uncommon in the days before central heating. "What do you think of the snow?"

Like so many, the entire family was agog at the introduction of trams within Hastings, and Alice, an older sister (Harriet) and their father were all photographed on the upper deck of the very first tram to run for the general public, this setting off from Silverhill at 7:20 a.m. on 31st July 1905. An early start! The day before, Alice had written excitedly to her future sister-in-law about the anticipated jaunt - by postcard, naturally - and on 1st August 1905, Annie wrote (loosely) on the reverse of a tram card, "Do you happen to know any of the folk aboard this tram? We do not think it's half bad. Hope you feel no ill-effects from your trip round. They are still passing here boarded inside and out". Not surprisingly, earlier in that same year when tram track-laying was in progress, appropriate postcards were circulated within the family with lively, questioning comments on the reverse. Mirror-writing was often used on postcards as security against prying eyes! Communication by postcard was highly useful at a time long before the telephone was in general use, and it must be remembered that the postal service was excellent. Often a card showing an event of local significance was chosen, and the reverse used to notify the recipient of some domestic detail such as musical entertainments enjoyed, the convenience of early motor-bus travel (Hastings being one of the first towns in the country to introduce such transport), and the huge novelty of the motor-car. On 7th September 1904, Alice wrote to a relative with the exciting news that her parents "have gone to Herstmonceux by motor. A motor on their own!" she scribbled, breathlessly. (See Pages 26 and 27 for tramway detail).

On 13th January 1906, Alice posted her future sister-in-law a card with a view of Silverhill, referring to "An open-air meeting on the *Pottery Ground* last night. Oh, it was packed, it was a Black Mass. H and myself are thinking of going down there Monday night to hear the Poll declared." The *Pottery Ground* was the site of the former Silverhill Pottery, off Sedlescombe Road North, and Alice was writing about the General Election of 1906. "H" referred to on the card was her sister, Harriet, and, as women, neither had the Vote. The open-air meeting in question was held by the Liberals (in the days before Radio and Television) and was indeed crowded according to the local Press. There were several such Public Meetings around the town during the Election campaign. On 15th January ("Monday" referred to by Alice) Polling Stations were open from 8 a.m. to 8 p.m. with the declaration of the Poll at about 11:15 p.m. from the Town Hall, close to the Cricket Ground. There was heavy rain during that evening, so the announcement was made to a large, but wet, crowd. The *Hastings Advertiser* of 11th January had said "As soon as the result is known, it will be telephoned to the various district police stations, so that those who prefer to stay at home may obtain the news at the earliest possible moment, and consequently may be prevented from coming in their thousands to swell the pressure in the centre of the town." I cannot imagine that either sister would have been deterred by rain, however heavy, on such an exciting evening and they probably heard the results announced at Silverhill, receiving a drenching in the process. No doubt they would have been accompanied by one of their brothers. The election was a victory for the Conservative candidate, Mr. Harvey du Cros. He defeated the sitting Liberal M.P. Mr. Freeman Freeman-Thomas who had won the seat in October 1900. Harvey du Cros resigned after being Hastings M.P. for only two years and was succeeded by his son, Arthur Philip du Cros, who served until 1918. (See Page 34).

At the time of the massive fire on board the German steamship *Lugano*, in April 1906, a card showing the blaze was duly despatched to a relative in Boreham Street with the following wording: "Thought you would like to have PPC of boat. Expect it will go tomorrow as they have unloaded it and tugged it out of the harbour." The unknown writer progressed then to more pressing concerns: "We have the painters in the house now. Have finished my kitchen today. Rather annoying to have all the upset again after having spring-cleaned it once. I have to be careful as the paint upsets me". Alice often posed little 'teasers' on the back of her cards. One such was sent to her future husband, Thomas Scrivens, postmarked 21st September 1909. She tells Tom that the picture on the card was taken on Hastings Pier the previous day, 20th September, and asks if he recognises anybody. Alice's mother, Ann Morris, is clearly identifiable within an interesting Pier scene showing an outing, probably from *St. Matthew's Church*, Silverhill, which featured prominently in the family's life. (See Pages 28 and 54).

In the past, everyone and everything seemed to be linked and inter-linked, other family surnames (apart from Scrivens and Morris) including Austin, Brett, Caister, Hunnisett (sometimes spelled "Honeysett"), Marchant and Sinden. Alice Morris's mother, Ann, (maiden name Hunnisett) had been born on Belle Hill, Bexhill Old Town, in 1845, dying in January 1919 as a result of the catastrophic influenza pandemic raging at that time. She and her many siblings remembered Samuel Scrivens and his family from *Millfield*, also on Belle Hill. Ann always spoke warmly of William and George Scrivens from Hastings (the last of the family to be remembered in the Crown Lane commemorative plaque, pictured on Page 194), George being particularly well-liked by the townspeople. Highly astute businessmen (William with his legal practice and George following their father - another William - into the *Hastings Old Bank*), they exerted considerable influence locally. Both endeavoured to put this influence to good use by being at the forefront of a number of social schemes and ventures at a time long before the introduction of the Welfare State. Conditions then cannot be compared fairly with those of today. *Scrivens Buildings*, intended originally to house fishing families needing to be near the Stade at a time when boats were dependent upon wind power, (and part of the *Hastings Cottage Improvement Society* established in 1857), is regarded by many as having been a form of early social housing. In Crown Lane, within the heart of the Old Town, it was, structurally, in advance of its day, being of ferro-concrete, and presented problems ultimately for the demolition-men in 1978.

Ann was vaccinated (possibly against smallpox, but strangely the certificate is not specific on this point) as a small child on 10th June 1847, the paperwork being issued by Frederick Wallis, Surgeon, who (like the Hunnisetts/Honeysetts) also lived on Belle Hill. (His son was to become heavily involved in Bexhill's struggle for improved sanitation following the typhoid epidemic of 1880). Subsequently the Honeysetts/Hunnisetts moved to Hastings Old Town, and Ann married Henry Morris at *St. Mary-in-the-Castle Church* in the 1860s. She sometimes spoke of her family's smuggling memories from past Belle Hill days in the very early 1800s, everyone within the local community being involved to some degree. Children then were "seen and not heard" but, on certain occasions they were, to their puzzled delight, encouraged to make as much noise as possible so that they were distracted and did not notice strange goings-on! A couple of brandy-testers serve as reminders of an often brutal occupation, now much romanticised. Len's copy of *Reminiscences of Smugglers and Smuggling*, by John Banks, (Master, *Parker Foundation*, later *Hastings Grammar School* and then *The William Parker School*) and dating from 1872/73, contains a description of the usage of similar glass beads when testing the strength of smuggled spirits. This little volume bears a hand-written inscription by the author to Charles Lockey who had a music saloon in Robertson Street, Hastings, at that time, the book being issued to coincide with a lecture delivered locally by John Banks.

Ann recounted, too, the probably apocryphal tale of the grocer whom she had known since he had been a young roundsman calling for orders when she was first married. Later he proclaimed on his fascia board that he was a fishermen's grocer. When asked how trade was doing, he replied, "I am a fishermen's grocer, and Hastings fishermen are an odd lot. Before they set out, they put a candle in the window. If it blows out, it's too rough. If it keeps alight, there isn't enough wind. So they don't go anyway!"

One of Ann's brothers, John Hunnisett (born 1848), was always referred to by Alice as "Uncle Jack" and, interestingly, L. J. Bartley in his book *The Story of Bexhill* mentions him thus:

> "At Bexhill, boating from the shore was a feature of the young resort in the later Victorian age, and the best-known vessel was *Skylark*, owned by Mr. James Gold who built the large seafront property between Sea and Brassey Roads. Earlier in life he had run supplies for the army in the Crimean War. By the early 1890s the bathing and boating station of Mr. John Hunnisett was popular; his obituary notice described him as a 'hard-working man much given to minding his own business and leaving other people alone', and when his funeral procession passed along the seafront the *Skylark's* flag was placed at half-mast. Hunnisett's bathing station, which became that of Ashworth and Hunnisett and was later acquired by the *Bexhill Bathing*

Company Limited, was originally built from the timbers of the sailing vessel *Isabella*, wrecked at Bexhill in 1883. In December 1910 the station was destroyed by a storm which carried the timbers out to sea whence they had come."

Photographs are shown of "Uncle Jack" in his beach "working" attire on Page 11.

I have already mentioned that my father, Leonard Scrivens, (an only child) had a great love of the town and, from an early age, he was allowed to roam freely, wherever he liked, without supervision. There seemed not to be the worries of today regarding children's personal safety. He was sent regularly to the Fishmarket to buy fish for home consumption, taking time to explore the Old Town and rambling over the East and West Hills as he wished. Provided his movements were known beforehand and he heeded instructions as to his time of return home, he was able to do much as he wanted. Undoubtedly this helped to instil self-reliance. Young Len is shown on Page 96: in later life on Page 188.

Many of Len's memories are of interest from a social and local history point of view. With his father, Tom, absent during the First World War, he and Alice, his mother, remained at his maternal grandparents' home in Silverhill, the area being, as previously indicated, very rural in those days. He remembered, as a youngster, picking (and eating) wild strawberries from the banks of Sedlescombe Road North, just south of Junction Road, when, as he put it, the most exciting traffic was the passing of a tram-car: two to the hour! He also picked spindlewood (both in flower and berry) from the footpath running from The Willows to Church Road, crossing the Hollington Stream, and cycled a great deal.

The family had many relatives in the surrounding country areas, particularly in Boreham Street (and not forgetting Herstmonceux where one of Tom's brothers lived). Normally the mode of transport to Boreham Street was by train to Pevensey and Westham, and being met there by horsedrawn governess cart for the remainder of the journey. On one occasion, however, long before the end of the War, Len went alone, aged about 5, by carrier's cart, picking this up at the *Star* Public House at Undercliff, St. Leonards, at 4:30 p.m. and arriving at Boreham Street between 8 and 9 o'clock. As he used to say, life certainly was leisurely then! Furthermore, in those days it was safe for children to travel unaccompanied - unlike today. With so many in the family (both by the sea and in the country) much use was made of carriers' carts, these being a highly popular and convenient way of transporting items such as flowers, fruit and vegetables. If someone experienced a glut, say of plums, others would benefit by using the carrier, a postcard advising them beforehand. "Thank you for the violets. They smelled lovely", was one typical response (by card), following a carrier's delivery.

Postcards show the stranded U-boat, U118, which was washed up opposite the *Queen's Hotel* on 15th April 1919, an occasion well-remembered by Len as it was his 8th birthday. The vessel was in the course of being taken from Harwich to Cherbourg for use by the French Navy when it broke tow in rough seas. The U-boat was later (with the help of the Fire Brigade) displayed to the public, the money raised going to charity. Cut up on the site, three dead German sailors were found, and later one or two of the men working on the wreck died as a result of the conditions within the hulk. On the same night, a second U-boat, part of the same tow, was washed up at Bulverhythe. Apparently the weather conditions were so severe that a small sailing coaster was beached at Breeds Place at the same time. (See Page 29).

Another of Len's memories was of a second beached coaster - presumably hit by a mine - around which he was rowed in the company of an aunt. He remembered the *Blimps* too: small airships which were stationed at Polegate, dive-bombing (presumably again mines) and one which got out of control and which, as he wrote, "draped itself with surrealistic effect across the whole frontage of the *Palace Pier*, St. Leonards". Another strong recollection concerned the Hastings Pier Fire of July 1917 (caused, it is thought, by a soldier's dropped cigarette). Written in 1978, it is reproduced, along with an unusual *Judge* bi-plane photograph of the sorry scene. (See Pages 30 and 31).

Again on a fire-fighting theme, Len's account of the almost unbelievable story of the massive conflagration at *Beauport* must be included here.

On the outskirts of St. Leonards, it had been the residence of General James Murray from about 1766 until his death in 1794. He became Governor of Quebec in 1760 and *Beauport* was named after a village near Quebec where Murray had been one of General Wolfe's three brigadiers, having been left in command after the French had surrendered. The property, largely rebuilt in about 1860, was gutted by fire in 1924 and was replaced by the present neo-Georgian house, which became an hotel.

"The estate is just outside the Borough boundary and when the alarm was raised the Battle Fire Brigade answered the call with their manual engine. Hastings had recently acquired a new motor-engine, *Diana*, housed at Shepherd Street, St. Leonards. This appliance also answered the call and made very good time but, on arrival, was refused access to nearby water by Battle, who claimed it was their fire. Further hose-reels were sent from Hastings as other water was distant on the well-wooded estate but, by then, the house had been reduced to a shell. Luckily, by 1940, we had the National Fire Service! The house had been the residence of Sir Archibald Lamb, and Great-Uncle George Brett (Parish Clerk of Hollington Church-in-the-Wood and of the prosperous monumental mason's business sited at Baldslow) was his Hollington Bailiff."

Brief mention must be made of the effect of the First World War on young Len and his family. His father, Thomas Scrivens, died at the age of 58 in 1942, his health ruined as a result of horrific experiences in France and Germany. Exhausted, he had been captured when the Germans attacked on 21st March 1918 - Tom just could not run fast enough. The German Officer giving chase motioned him to sit down on a wall, took a few paces back, and reached inside his jacket pocket. Naturally, Tom feared the worst, thinking his last moment had come and that he would be shot. He could not believe his eyes when a camera was produced and he was photographed! In a way he was "shot" and I often wonder where that "snap" finally came to rest. Tom's life as a Private in the Machine Gun Corps, and subsequently as a prisoner-of-war, was horrendous, and the conditions endured by him (and by many others) were appalling. The official "missing" letter from Captain Boyle is reproduced in full on Page 16. Dated 8th April, it arrived in Silverhill on 12th April - Tom's 34th birthday - Alice carefully noting the date of receipt on the reverse of the envelope. Len was just three days away from his 7th birthday and Alice had been due to celebrate her 34th birthday on 25th April. Here is an extract from Tom's first letter home, scribbled in pencil:

"I am glad to tell you I am getting along as well as can be expected, it being very different from the busy life I have had since we came to France. It is just two weeks today *(Tom's letter is dated 4th April 1918)* since we were taken prisoner and I hope I shall never experience another 21st March like that. One day I shall be able to tell you all about it.

I lost all my belongings and have only just what I stand up in - razor, underclothes, etc., all gone. We were issued with a little bit of soap today so must get a wash now. I have one handkerchief which does as a towel. We had a good bath the other morning, our heads shaved, clothes fumigated, and I can tell you we felt better for it. No livestock now.

There are 250 of us in this huge hut and about 10 of the original company that was with me at Belton and we all lie side by side so we talk of the good times we have had. The time seems so long here. You see, we are so isolated, there being all nationalities the other side of the wire. There are quite a few of our own boys. I met a chap out of the Rifle Brigade that knew me in the City.

They say when we get over the other side, we shall get parcels from the Red Cross. I don't think the Government allows you to send these in personally - they all have to come through the Societies (I could do with one though). I can receive as many letters as you like to send so let the others know my address and perhaps they will drop me a line.

I am pleased the better weather is coming. Let's hope the War will soon be over, and then home again - what say you? I hope Len is well - give him a hug from Dad. I hope mother is about again now. My love to Mrs. Hayday *(Mrs. Ann Hayday, who had married into the well-known Victorian Craft Book-Binding firm, Hayday, and by then widowed, lived with the Morris family, she and her late husband having previously retired to St. Leonards)*, and the others. (See Page 187).

Now don't you worry about me for we are being treated quite all right and we must both look forward to the homecoming. I don't know how long this letter will take, but I shall send all of them to you and now I shall look for some bumper ones from home. You could make enquiries about the parcels."

It is not difficult to imagine the reaction in St. Leonards following the arrival of Tom's letter. Desperately needed food parcels, although sent, never arrived and at one stage, being forced to work in a salt-mine, Tom survived simply due to the consumption of quantities of salt which he hid in his pockets, this practice naturally contributing to dire health problems in later years. Meanwhile, back home in St. Leonards, everyone had become accustomed to hearing the sound of gunfire when the wind was in the right direction, this seeming to emphasise how near, and yet so far away, were many loved ones. How happy Tom was when, following the cessation of hostilities, he arrived home on 3rd January 1919, travelling on a Danish ship where everything was spotless and where he was able to enjoy the "luxury" of clean sheets. Perhaps "happy" is not the right word, as the joy surrounding Tom's return was severely clouded by the fact that Alice's mother, Ann Morris, had died the previous day, 2nd January, as already discussed on Page 20. There had been other bad news, too, Tom's father, William Scrivens, having also died (the year before, in 1918), his burial being in Dorking. Alice's father died in 1924 aged 78. Not surprisingly, the war years took their toll and subsequently Tom was frequently extremely ill. As an aside, wherever he had been based during the War, both in England and France, Tom's culinary expertise was exploited. He was always drafted in personally to prepare meals for the Officers, using only the very best ingredients and produce available. The wastage involved was shameful (noticeably so at Seaford), particularly bearing in mind the deprivations suffered by so many at that time. Bound copies of Annual Reports for the East Sussex Hospital, opposite Hastings Pier, and covering the First World War years, give a detailed insight into the workings of the Hospital at a particularly difficult period. This was prior to the establishment of the new facility in Cambridge Road, and long before the introduction of the National Health Service. (See Pages 146 and 147).

On a happier note, from an early age Len derived much pleasure from local secondhand book-shops (of which there were many). His first purchase, as a small boy in the very early 1920s, was a copy of *Hastings and Environs - A Sketch-Book* by H. G. Hampton, published by A. & C. Black in 1915. Realising (and encouraging) Len's interest in local history, his introduction to *Hastings Museum* (then sited within the *Brassey Institute* in Claremont) came about as the result of a visit, in the company of his Aunt Nell, to an exhibition of watercolour drawings, illustrating a century's changes in Old Hastings. This was held in December/January 1923/4, and featured works by Brooke and Badham. The Museum publication for this exhibition was priced at two (old) pence! He retained many happy memories following the transfer to John's Place, along with a number of (now browning) Museum publications dating from the 1930s onwards. The earliest family Museum publication, well-illustrated and dating from 1909, for an exhibition on Local Antiquities, cost one shilling. Len later frequented the *Old Town Hall Museum* (established after the Second World War) and (from 1956) the *Fishermen's Museum* (opened as a Church in 1854).

(See Pages 4, 20, 65, 68, 78, 97, 137, 193, plus Appendix on Page 187, for bookish memories, including recollections of local booksellers).

——◆◇▶——

Above & Below: **Record Snow Storm, Hastings, 30th December 1908.** Eastwards (above), Westwards (below). Oxo much needed. One very suspicious snow-clearer!

Above & Below: Heavy snow over Old Town and over "new" Hastings, 3rd March 1909.

HEAVY SNOW, HASTINGS, 3rd **March 1909.**
(See weather comments for 1879 and early 1900s on Pages 18/19).

Above left: Old London Road
Below left: Alexandra Park

Above right: High Street
Below right: Queen's Road

The four cards on this page show the laying of Tram-Lines prior to the introduction of Trams in Hastings in 1905. (See Page 19).

Above left: Silverhill.

Below left: Hughenden Road.

Above right: Bohemia Road.

Below right: London Road, Ore.

Above & below: **Official Tram Trial Trip** - 15th July 1905, Silverhill and Memorial. Lady, below left, oblivious to excitement. (See tramway memories on Page 19).

Above & below: **First Public Tram Run** - 31st July 1905, Silverhill. Tram left at 7.20 a.m. Morris family members visible on top deck. Upper scene at 7.10 a.m.

FIRST TRAM TO RUN IN HASTINGS. July 15th, 1905. "Judge" Series.

S.S. LUGANO=ON=FIRE LYING=IN=HASTINGS HARBOUR SCOTT 27-4-06.

On 26th April 1906, **The Steamship Lugano** was travelling from Baltimore to Hamburg with a mixed cargo, including oil and timber. (See Page 19).

She also carried cotton which self-ignited causing a catastrophic fire. Hastings lifeboat Charles Arkcoll II assisted. A caption within the "multi-scene" card reads, simply, "Unbearable".

JUDGE-PHOTO.

S.S. LUGANO ON FIRE OFF HASTINGS. APRIL 28/06.

HASTINGS LIFEBOAT RENDERING ASSISTANCE

THE CAPTAIN

UNBEARABLE

THE HOLD

SCENES ON BOARD S.S. LUGANO ON FIRE APRIL 26

A TWISTED MAST

The stranded **German U-Boat, 118,** washed up opposite the Queen's Hotel, 15th April 1919 due to abnormal weather conditions.

Details of this, and of other incidents on that date, may be found on Page 21.

HASTINGS PIER DESTROYED BY FIRE A written memory left by Leonard Scrivens (1911 - 1992)

15th July, 1917, was a Sunday and I remember it well. In the afternoon I had gone for a walk with Aunt Nell (E.M. Morris). Probably at my request, we headed for the abandoned quarry/brickyard at the top of Red Lane (now Harrow Lane) - in those days unmade but with one terrace of twelve houses (Red Cottages) on the south side. From the high ground we saw a mass of smoke from the seafront area and hurried home to find out what was wrong.

We learned that the Pier was ablaze and, with grandfather (H. Morris) and my mother (A. Scrivens), hastened to White Rock where we had a good view from the rising ground at the side of the Hospital. There was a huge crowd (Hastingers always enjoy a free show) and we could easily see Uncle Harry Morris and his fellow-firemen at their work. The fire, however, was gaining, forcing a continual retreat as it crept along the decking under the firemen's feet, and quite early on grandfather declared that the only way to beat it would be to cut a firebreak. This was eventually done, but not before everything up to the almost new Parade extension had been destroyed.

The Hastings Fire Brigade was then, and until the last War, a voluntary body (really a sort of tradesmen's club) and the following will emphasise how amateur things were.

Early in the afternoon of the 15th July, all appliances were called out. The Silverhill section fire engine was kept at Battle Road adjacent to Ellis Bros. timber yard, this firm's heavy draught horses always being used, but it was a Sunday (the day of rest) and the horses were not available. Herbert Till, Foreman-in-Charge, did not hesitate - he, a man of decision, commandeered a passing tramcar, the fire engine with steam getting up was attached, and thus the firemen, in comfort, proceeded to what was certainly the Brigade's biggest fire.

The devastation was complete and after a week or so the Fire Brigade formed a catwalk to the pier-head and, for a small fee, would escort parties to view, the proceeds being passed to charities. I was taken and, thereafter, had a recurring and very unpleasant dream in which I was caught by the sea on the Pier when making for land - I always woke up before things reached a climax!

Incidentally, the biplane in the photograph was sent by the military at Dover to see what all the smoke was about. Presumably, in 1917 Dover Castle was still without a telephone!

Judge photograph, imprint in bottom left corner. (See Pages 21 and 31).

VOLUNTEER FIRE BRIGADE

Above: Harry (Henry Charles) Morris - 1875-1932. Volunteer Fireman, pictured in his uniform in November, 1916.

Above right: Harry (third from right), a member of the Silverhill Fire Brigade crew. Pictured, c. 1912, with his colleagues and their highly-decorated horse-drawn vehicle. Note the over-large "helmet" aloft and the dummy "fireman" up a ladder at the rear.
Perhaps about to participate in a celebratory parade.

Below right: Card published by F.J. Parsons Ltd., showing aftermath of catastrophic Hastings Pier Fire, 15th July 1917, Harry being one of the firemen involved. (See Pages 21 and 30).

68 HASTINGS. — The Hospital. — LL.

Above: East Sussex Hastings & St. Leonards Hospital, now site of White Rock Theatre (formerly Pavilion), opposite Hastings Pier, photographed by Louis Levy.
Below & to left: Triumphal Arch erected by Hastings firemen in Warrior Square (Edinburgh Hotel) in honour of visit by H.R.H. The Duchess of Albany 1st April 1913. She opened a Bazaar (lasting three days) which raised money for the Hospital Removal Fund in connection with the planned transfer to Cambridge Road (eventually the Royal East Sussex Hospital).

Above: St. Leonards Pier Shop - gale damage, 26th/27th Nov. 1905. Judge card.

Below: Denmark Place storm damage - 26th November 1905.

Above: "Silhouette" shot - Hastings storm, 10th December 1908.

Below: Hastings Harbour - gale damage, 22nd October 1911.

Above: A crowded town-centre scene on Election Day, 1906, with Albert Memorial in background. Much excitement locally and a victory for Conservative candidate, Harvey du Cros, who resigned after two years and was succeeded by his son, Arthur Philip du Cros, who served until 1918. (See Page 19 for memories).

GENERAL ELECTION - 1906
SUFFRAGETTE DEMONSTRATION - c. 1913
SUFFRAGETTE ACTION - 1913

Below left: Suffragette demonstration, possibly 1913. Queen's Road, Hastings, strategically close to Town Hall. (One sandwich-board reads: "Stop Forcible Feeding").

Below right: Card depicting the aftermath of the burning by Suffragettes, on 15th April 1913, of the du Cros family home, Levetleigh, Dane Road, St. Leonards.

THE SALVATION ARMY IN HASTINGS

Above: Marching along South Terrace, Hastings - c. 1920s.
Below: Marching down Queen's Road, Hastings - c. 1920s.

Above: Collecting funds, probably in 1908 as card posted in Hastings in February 1909. Poster on hand-cart reads: "Proceeds for poor children's teas on New Year's Day". (Although hard to believe now, in the 1880s the Salvation Army in Hastings had to endure violence from certain local groups, this being common in other areas, too, and *not* confined to Hastings). Is seasonal music still played outside Albany Court on Christmas Day morning?

Above: Memorial area flooded - 22nd October 1911.

Above: Cricket Ground flooded - 23rd March 1913. Originally medieval harbour site.

Below: Parade Storm damage - 18th November 1911.

Below: Memorial area flooded - 23rd March 1913.

80. PARADE. HASTINGS.   PHOTO BY JUDGES'

JUDGE-PHOTO.   58.   A WET DAY ON THE FRONT
HASTINGS.

SUN, SHOWERS, SNOW, STORM!

Four Judge cards, all pre-First War.

Hastings - Looking eastwards, with the Bandstand on the left.
(The Bandstand was moved to White Rock Gardens in the late 1920s.)

468. SNOW AT HASTINGS.   JUDGES.

6. STORM AT HASTINGS.
SEPT. 1ST. 1908.
PHOTO BY JUDGES'

Left: **Hastings Fishmarket** on dank, foggy day in early 1900s. Note two women and schoolboys.

Below left: **"Tubbing"** at Hastings, early 1900s. Traditional washtub antics at sea. Donations later collected from crowds watching on beach.

Below right: Alfred Mills "Biddy" Stonham, 1879-1964, fisherman, lifeboatman and last Hastings Tubman.

His act required great strength and skill, and sometimes young ladies were invited to actively participate in the entertainment. He continued fishing and tubbing until 1963. A great character, he was also extremely courageous, being presented with the RNLI Silver Medal for bravery in 1904 by King Edward VII.

Above & Below: External and internal views of Fishermen's Church, opened in 1854. Since 1956, the Fishermen's Museum. Early 1900s.
(Note horse with his master at left of upper card).

Above: Fishermen's huts, also known as Net Shops, Old Town, plus capstan horses.

Below: Perhaps the oldest Hastings shell stall? Card posted 1905.

THE IMPORTANCE OF THE HORSE

Mr. Dick Russell, Riding and Job Master, and Livery Stable Keeper, etc., St. Andrew's Mews, Queen's Road, and The Gables, Wellington Mews, Hastings, also King's Road Mews, St. Leonard's.—About eight years ago Mr. Dick Russell commenced business in a comparatively small way, as job master and fly proprietor at Harold Mews, East Ascent, and now he owns three large mews in Hastings and St. Leonards, and controls one of the best businesses of its kind in the district. This is in itself sufficient evidence of the energy, enterprise, and ability with which the business has been conducted, and of the efficient manner in which Mr. Dick Russell has catered for the public requirements in this respect. The original premises have been relinquished as entirely inadequate and unsuitable to the greatly increased business, and the mews now occupied are commodious, well appointed, and conveniently situated in central and accessible positions in St. Leonards and Hastings, while the order office at 1, Stockleigh Road, which is in direct communication with the yards and stables, enables orders from all parts of the town to be executed with the greatest possible promptitude. The St. Andrew's Mews face the cricket ground, and the Wellington Mews are only a short distance off, while the King's Road Mews are close to Warrior Square, and the three sets of premises afford great

Mr. Dick Russell: *Left:* From "Views & Reviews - Special Edition - Hastings", W.T. Pike & Co., 1897.
Above: Postcard by Francis Frith & Co. Ltd., Reigate.
Below: Horses, bicycles, motor-cars, tram-lines. November 1908 visit by Lord Mayor of London, Sir George Wyatt Truscott, of 100 Marina, St. Leonards, by Judge premises, then at 42 White Rock. (Re: visit to Buchanan Hospital).

accommodation, close on fifty horses and ponies being owned at present by Mr. Dick Russell, while ample accommodation is also provided for horses and carriages standing at livery. The stables are well constructed with spacious well appointed stalls and loose boxes, the ventilation and sanitary arrangements being of a highly efficient character, and the whole place including yards, harness-rooms, and coach-houses, is kept in apple-pie order, the strictest cleanliness prevailing throughout. Well horsed carriages and vehicles of all kinds can be promptly supplied in first class style, perfectly appointed in every detail, and in charge of careful and experienced drivers; brakes, waggonettes, private carriages, dog carts, phaetons, etc., being always available on the shortest notice for drives, private pleasure parties, picnics, excursions, weddings, and other occasions. The most careful attention is given to hunters and other horses at livery, none but thoroughly trustworthy men being allowed about the stables. The charges throughout are also very moderate. At the last horse and carriage parade, Mr. Dick Russell was successful in obtaining the first and second prizes for four horse char-a-bancs and pair horse brakes, and during the summer months, he runs three well appointed four horse char-a-bancs, viz: "The Nonpareil," "Victoria," and "Reliance," to all the places of interest in the neighbourhood of Hastings. He is exceedingly popular in the district and his already extensive connection is rapidly increasing.

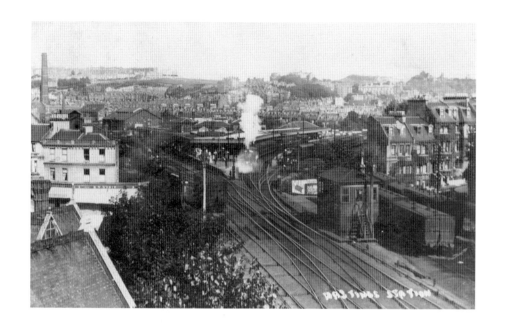

THE STEAM RAILWAY, MOTOR-CAR, AND HORSE

Left: Hastings Station from Linton Road bridge. A good head of steam! (See Pages 90, 91 and 182).

Below left: Motor Parade, 26th June 1907, travelling westwards. Car No. 35 is passing James Jenner and Son, bootmakers, next door to Cave, Austin & Co., auctioneers, adjacent to Cave, Austin, grocers, all on Grand Parade, St. Leonards. Car No. 35 is so heavily decorated florally that, although the steering-wheel is just visible, the driver is virtually hidden from view!

Below: Hastings & St. Leonards Horse Parade - 12th May 1913. Justifiably proud Mr. Henry Miller of Oxford House, St. Saviour's Road, St. Leonards, is surrounded by his admiring supporters, with his beautifully decorated "entry". Note horse's floral head-dress.

MOTOR PARADE JUNE 26TH 1907.   HASTINGS.

Don't forget to visit JEPSON'S Extensive Showrooms,
12 ROBERTSON STREET.

HASTINGS AND ST. LEONARDS
LEADS THE WAY WITH MOTOR 'BUSES AND SUNSHINE.

PRINTED & PUBLISHED BY KING BROS., STATIONERS, &c.

VERY EARLY MOTOR-BUS ADVERTISING CARDS
Above and below: Pair of Jepson's Advertising cards.

Above: Warrior Square bus advertises King's Library; Skinner & Co. Ltd. Note edge detail regarding sunshine and outside passengers.

Below: Advertisement for Plummer Roddis Ltd; in window for "Royal Austrian Band" at both Hastings and St. Leonards Piers.

Don't forget to visit JEPSON'S Extensive Showrooms,
12 ROBERTSON STREET.

TWO FURTHER FORMS OF TRANSPORT

Right: Motor Ambulance - St. John Ambulance Brigade, Hastings Corps. Back and front of card, postally used, 4th October 1917.

Below: Trolley-bus pictured outside *The Victoria Inn*, Battle Road, St. Leonards. Illustration and caption from *50 Years of Service*, Maidstone & District Motor Services Ltd., 1961.

One of the 57-seater Guy trolley-buses of the Hastings Tramways Company, which replaced the trams in 1928.

A STRANGE MOTOR-BUS ACCIDENT
IN HASTINGS

A STRANGE JOURNEY –
THROUGH HASTINGS
ON FOOT

Above: This empty motor-bus was involved in an accident in Havelock Road at about 9 o'clock on Tuesday morning, 22nd August 1905. In an attempt to avoid a collision with a barrow, the bus crashed into a mound of earth at a spot where drains' work was being carried out. Another bus soon arrived: a chain was attached and the vehicle dragged off to continue on its way - presumably the driver was uninjured. Interested spectators and caped policeman. Part of the offices of the officially known Rape of Hastings Mutual Permanent Benefit Building Society can be seen in the background. In 1908 the title was shortened to that of Hastings Permanent Building Society. (Earlier premises are shown on Page 92).

Right: **"Iron Mask", Hastings, 1st February 1908.**
Harry Bensley, a well-known "chancer", accepted a wager of $100,000 (then £21,000, and now £1·5 million), from American J.P. Morgan (founder of J.P. Morgan Bank) and Lord Lonsdale. He had to walk round the world wearing an iron helmet, pushing a perambulator, and finding a wife en route, existing entirely on the sale of publicity postcards. Charles Tipton accompanied Bensley to ensure he never revealed his identity. Setting off from Trafalgar Square on 1st January 1908, and supposedly travelling for six years, Bensley eventually received £4,000, having bought his first pair of new boots in Hastings. It is now believed that the stunt was a confidence trick, the journey being a forfeit after the eccentric lost his fortune in a card-game.

MOTORING, WALKING AND BALLOONING

Left: The New Battle of Hastings - 17th March, 1909

Gist of wording taken from card panel:

On this date Hastings was once more invaded, an imaginary enemy having landed and destroyed the Railway. The Automobile Association solved the problem of transport and furnished a large number of Motor Cars for the conveyance of Troops to the Front. A Battalion of Guards consisting of upwards of 1,000 officers and men (under the command of Lt.-Col. Erskine) together with their Machine Guns, Ammunition, Blankets, Food, Water, Medical and all other requisite stores were conveyed from London to Hastings, a distance of 54 miles, nearly 500 Cars being used in connection with this important event.

Below left: Original brick-built St. Andrew's Arch, top of Queen's Road, replaced 1898 by iron railway bridge, known as Queen's Bridge. Note advertising signs and suspicious pedestrians.

Below: Ballooning over Alexandra Park. Lawn Tennis match in progress, plus plenty of deck-chairs.

EAST HILL LIFT

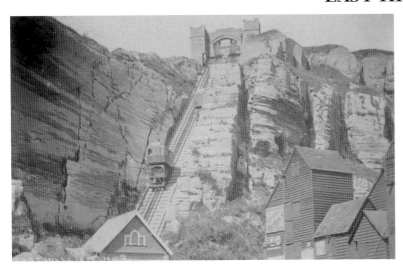

Opened in 1902, the steepest line in southern England, with outstanding views. Advertising sign for outfitter Felton Smith of High Street, Old Town.

Above: Lift in distance; Lifeboat house behind schoolboys; washing on shingle.

Below: Curious spectators, some (including baby) aware of photographer.

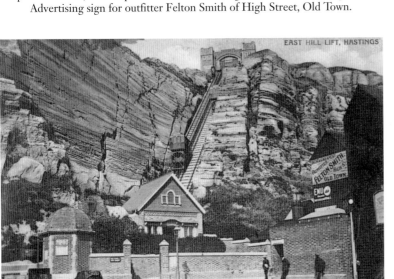

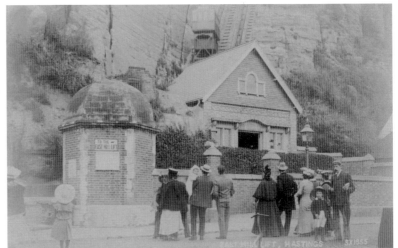

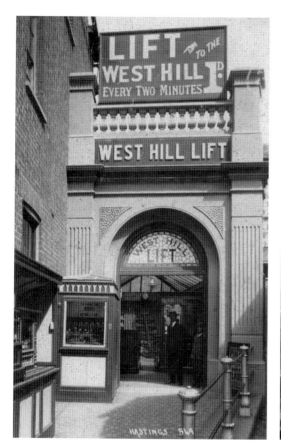

WEST HILL LIFT opened 1891 and running largely through a tunnel.

Cost and frequency of journey shown, (early 1900s), plus proud lift-men with lift, and queue of eager passengers, including small boy aware of photographer, as is attendant by cash register (possibly the same person as the standing man on the middle card). Advertising sign for furniture dealer Edwin Smith who had impressive premises at East Hill House in Rock-a-Nore Road. Splendid views from top of hill.

BICYCLING / PHOTOGRAPHY

Harry (Henry Charles) Morris (1875 - 1932), a member of the St. Leonards Cycling Club, wearing cap sporting its Badge. Photograph taken c. 1896 by J.H. Blomfield, Trinity House, 44 Robertson Street, Hastings. Harry is listed as being present at the 1896 St. Leonards Cycling Club Dinner featured on opposite page.

Blomfield & Co., as it became, was one of the oldest firms of photographers connected with Hastings. Originally established by Messrs. Ayles and Bonniwell in 1857, the firm passed into the hands of Blomfield in 1867 and the business rapidly expanded. Embracing every type of portraiture work, they and their predecessors were favoured by people from all walks of life and all classes of society, many names, including that of H.R.H. The Prince of Wales, being quoted within "Views & Reviews, Special Edition, Hastings" published 1897 by W.T. Pike. The Ashburnham, Brassey, and De La Warr families are mentioned, too, as well as the artists Sydney Cooper and Harry Furniss. In Pike's Directory for 1894, Mr. J.H. Blomfield advertised "Special Evening Photography by the Electric Light. Hours - Mondays, Wednesdays, Thursdays and Saturdays, from 7 p.m. to 10 p.m." The premises were obviously lush, judging by the two photographs reproduced below and taken from the "Views & Reviews" publication.

(See also Pages 13, 18, 49 and 50 for textual detail as to the social significance of the bicycle).

Reception-room

The Studio

HASTINGS, ST. LEONARDS & BEXHILL

AMUSEMENTS

AND VISITORS' GUIDE.

A WEEKLY PROGRAMME OF FORTHCOMING EVENTS,

Review of Local News, Corporation Band Programme, Walks, Drives, Train Service, Excursions, Etc.

WISHING YOU A HAPPY CHRISTMAS

To the right and below are extracts from the *Hastings, St. Leonards & Bexhill Amusements and Visitors' Guide* (priced at one penny) for week commencing Monday November 16th 1896.

ON Wednesday the annual dinner of the St. Leonards Cycling Club took place at the Royal Concert Hall, St. Leonards, one of the largest rooms at the rear of the stage being utilised for the purpose. Alderman Weston, (the Mayor) presided, and the company included: H. Kenward, F. Williard (Captain), F. Watkins, Wingfield (2), A. Monk, T. A. Noakes (sub-captain of the Hastings Cycling Club), A. Turner, Smith (2). E. Head, F. Bridgland (sub-captain), R. Tremble, W. G. Elphick (hon-sec.), S. W. Allen, E. Creed, C. Gilham, H. Morris, R A Grant, F.M. Kenny, C. Head, C.W. Miller, W. Mills, D. Rollason, H. Tolhurst, G. Lambkin, H. Philpot, W. Beaney, F. Rymill, S. Smith, E. Cruttenden, J. Blackman, G. Hide, and F. F. Nash.—After dinner the Mayor gave the loyal toasts, and Mr. H. Kenward submitted "The Mayor and Corporation." They deeply appreciated the presence of the Mayor. His presence showed how high cycling was held in the estimation of the general public.

(See facing Page).

Left: 1881 Christmas card showing acrobatic, pipe-smoking cyclist.

INFORMATION TO CYCLISTS.

Ladies' Skirts should not be more than 2¼ yards round, nor nearer the ground than four to five inches. Elastic bands, to button on the inside of the shoe from the dress, should be used. Avoid tight lacing.

Never ride within half-an-hour of a meal, either before or after.

A bell or alarm is compulsory, and must be sounded on overtaking horses, vehicles, pedestrians, etc. The mere ringing of a bell gives no right of way, but is only used as a warning. Speak coaxingly to restive horses, and pass led horses on the off or led side.

It is compulsory by Act of Parliament to have a lighted lamp at night. Use the best oil, and renew wick frequently. Ireland has no local Government Act requiring the use of either lamp or bell, and there are no bye-laws in force.

Keep to your own side of the road ; if not, you must use more care, but do not think that others who are not must pay the penalty if any accident happens. Departure from the rule of the road is only allowable when departing from it will actually avoid accident.

Do not ride on footpaths that run along the highway, or you are liable to a fine, and remember that pedestrians have a prior right to the road, and are not compelled to get out of the way, even if you give due warning of your approach. Riding beyond ten miles an hour is punishable. Where two or more are riding furiously, each one is liable if an accident is caused by any of them.

Cyclists who leave machines in care of hotel ostlers, etc., must constitute themselves guests, or they cannot recover for loss or damage.

A brake should never be dispensed with by the road rider or tourist. The absence of brake or alarm is evidence against you in case of accident.

Oil frequently, and only a little at a time; avoid extremes. Viscoleum is recommended. When oiling it is a good plan to try all nuts with your fingers, to see if any have become loose, and so that both gearings may be lubricated, lean machine first on the right, then on the left. Keep oil off your tyres.

Oil your chain as follows : Take off occasionally, wash out the grit in paraffin or benzoline, dry, then immerse in lubricating oil, gearoleum, or viscoleum, or paint chain with black lead, mixed in methylated spirits; wipe quite dry, and refix. See that the chain is neither too tight nor too slack.

Have the bearings so adjusted that the wheels, etc., spin freely, but without any perceptible side-shake. Bearings never require taking to pieces to clean ; run paraffin or benzoline through them while spun.

Tyres moderately inflated give the best results. If too hard, the hot sun will burst them. If too soft, they will get nipped between the road and the rim. After repairing, slightly inflate the air chamber; it will go in easier, and prevent nipping.

Saddle soreness is sometimes alleviated by tilting or adjusting the saddle, or by shortening the crank.

When the roads are slippery, work the pedals smoothly, as jerky pedalling may cause a side slip.

Cyclists should have plain, wholesome food, and avoid gassy or alcoholic drinks. When thirsty, stone pop, lime juice, bovril, and plenty of fruit is recommended by the faculty. Try rinsing the mouth with cold water; take fluids sparingly.

For frosty winter riding, use two pairs of stockings, two sweaters, gaiters, woollen gloves, with your sleeves tucked into them, and an ear cap; and breathe only through your nostrils. Don't leave your lamp outside when not in use, or the oil will freeze. Frost makes mild steel very brittle; so ride carefully.

Woollen garments should always be worn next to the skin.

Before putting your machine away, see that the bright parts are dry and well vaselined or silico enamelled, and store in a dry place; you may ruin your machine by neglect. Cork handles may be made to look as clean as new by rubbing with a piece of rag saturated in alcohol.

If you have not floor space for storing, fix a pulley and cord in the ceiling, and wind it up; by using two pulleys the machine will hang flat against the ceiling.

VICTORIAN CHRISTMAS CARDS - BICYCLING "CRAZE"

Left: Concertina-style card. When fully opened, two lady cyclists are revealed. Verse within. 1890s.

Below: Concertina-style card, fully opened here, showing three cycling postmen approaching a housemaid. When closed, only one postman apparent. Verse on back. 1890s.

Right: "The Lady Scorcher" is being chased by a male admirer. 1890s. The term "Scorcher" was a reference to some of the more reckless and speedy cyclists. Bicycling played a not inconsiderable role in the run-up to women's emancipation, their clothing needing to be adapted for reasons of safety and practicality, this causing a furore in certain quarters.

Below right: The smallest card consists of a "scrap" stuck onto card - often the way then. On reverse is written "Xmas 1877".

VICTORIAN CHRISTMAS CARDS - ICE-SKATING AND BOOT-MAKING

A Merry Christmas

Left: Elaborate hand-made card. Layers of velvet cut to form skater's costume and muff. Lace trim to skirt. Velvet "skates", etc. Tiny floral brooch on jacket lapel. Skater's head, with hat and flowers in hair, is a "scrap", c. 1870s.

Right: Ice-skating young ladies (and boy in sailor-suit). All, naturally, are hatted, c. 1890s.

Below: The Victorians were very keen on word-play and these two cards, based around the subject of boot-making, display examples of this passion. The boot and tools on the left-hand card form a "scrap" stuck onto the card. Published by Angus Thomas of London, noted for comic cards using all manner of puns and spelling tricks. Both c. 1890s.

WISHING YOU A HAPPY CHRISTMAS.

With Hearty Wishes that You may know
WHERE TO REPAIR.
(within a FOOT or two)
for A JOLLY CHRISTMAS
and may You PEG away merrily with
plenty of BRADS in the NEW YEAR.

There are many get *soled*
o'er their Christmas delights,
But their feelings are easy to *heel*,
For their *waxy* derangement
of temper won't *last*,
When a *patch* of good humour they feel.

May you make a *good job* of the frolic and fun
That *sow* with the gayest you'll shout,
And *awl* the good things that you want may you get,
And may none of 'em ever wear out!

ANGUS THOMAS   COPYRIGHT NO. 166   LONDON

(See Page 18 for 1879 and early 1900s ice-skating and boot-making detail).

A Happy Christmas to you.

Some people WAX gloomy, and cheerless, and glum,
For directly the Summer has passed,
When they speak of the Happy New Year that's to come,
Say, "It wont be A PATCH ON THE LAST,"
But we'll hope for the best, now that Christmas is here
And we won't be depressed or let troubles annoy
So accept my kind Greeting and Wishes Sincere
That your heart may be glad and your SOLE full of joy.

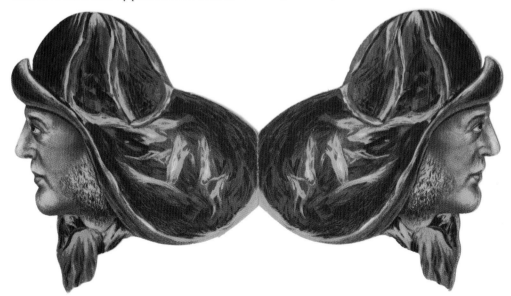

VICTORIAN CHRISTMAS CARDS

Christmas & New Year card, 1860s, published by Goodall. Comic verse on back by Alfred Crowquill. Alfred Henry Forrestier used this name jointly with his brother, Charles Robert, one drawing, the other writing. This illustration is probably by A.H. Forrestier.

Above: Lifeboat-shaped Christmas card, c. 1880, (not a Hastings boat). Design repeated on back. Opens up to reveal seascape, seasonal greetings, and verse by Johnston Beall (active at that date). Metallic anchor. No mention of Royal status of National Lifeboat Institution. Publisher and designer unknown.

Below: Opened-out, shaped, late Victorian Christmas card of Fisherman's Head. Publisher unknown. Fishing illustrations within by T.R. Kennedy who worked for Eyre & Spottiswoode 1878-87. Festive verse by prolific Helen Marion Burnside (born 1843).

The Oyster and Cod Fish

A native oyster, quite a swell,
He'd just got out of bed,
Met an old cod fish walking out
With such a jolly head.

"How do, fine fellow, this fine morn?"
The oyster cried aloud;
The cod fish started with amaze,
For he was rather proud.

"Why! drat you, fellow," he replied,
"To stop me on my way;
What can a block of shell like you
To me pretend to say?"

"What!" cried the oyster, "jolter head!
You needn't be so cross;
For what would you be worth without
I helped you with my sauce?"

Above: *The Welcome Stranger* Public House, Sedlescombe Road North. 1909 Harvest Festival Collection for Buchanan Hospital.

Below: King's Road Christmas lights - published pre-1908 by J.J. Samuels Ltd.

Above: Rural Sedlescombe Road, c. 1906. Tram; Beagley's Auction Hoarding for Hollington House and Silverhill Lodge. See Page 60 for detail on Beagley's.

Below: Battle Road, Hollington, 1908, lively scene. Dorrie Morris, later Coleman, aged 10, in large white hat, outside W. Harmer.

HASTINGS PIER

Left: On Hastings Pier - picture taken 20th September 1909. (At height of the postcard "craze", mirror-writing was often favoured as an aid to privacy and Alice Morris, later Scrivens, sometimes decorated the reverse of her cards with small, silhouette sketches). Very likely this card shows a group outing from St. Matthew's Church, Silverhill. Alice's mother wears a splendid hat, as was the custom then. Note deck-chair seating. "Chocolates and Sweets - All the Best Makes" is the advertisement wording. Note child at extreme left, not paying attention to the camera, whilst dog snoozes peacefully on extreme right! Six months earlier, the Pier was covered with heavy snow. (See Page 19).

Below left: Entrance to Hastings Pier - card posted 1904, prior to introduction of trams in 1905. Boer War Memorial of 1903 in background. Note lady wheeling highly elaborate baby-carriage (on left). She is obviously linked with the little girl (in sturdy boots) who is standing close to (possibly) her mother or an older sister. "Mother" is staring intently at the camera, whereas the little girl is more interested in something on the Pier which has caught her eye. The hoarding at the entrance advertises performances, in the Pier Pavilion, of Dickens's "The Cricket on the Hearth", one of the most successful of his Christmas books.

Below right: An example of entertainment on Hastings Pier prior to the First War - Professor Davenport's Bicycle Dive. Curious spectators.

ST. LEONARDS PIER - All Judge cards

Above: View from Pier - early 1900s. *Below:* Roller-skating on Pier - early 1900s.
Below right: Hastings & St. Leonards Winter Orchestra - Opening Ceremony on Pier - 18th January 1908. Flashlight photography used by Fred Judge. A very fulsome report appeared in the Hastings & St. Leonards Observer of 25th January 1908, at the end of which it was stated that copies of this photograph could be obtained from Messrs. Judge's, then at White Rock.

"In spite of foggy weather, a fashionable audience crowded the pavilion". "The crimson draperies and red-shaded lamps gave a luxurious touch, which was heightened by numerous palms and flowers. The surroundings were very cosy and, though the seating accommodation was taxed to its fullest capacity, everybody was in good humour."

The Opening Ceremony took place at 3 p.m., with many dignitaries present including The Mayor, Alderman R.W. Mitchell, J.P.; Alderman B.H.W. Tree (Chairman of the Entertainments Association); Mr. Harvey du Cros, J.P., M.P.; and Mrs. Harvey du Cros. The orchestral programme, (very detailed) was *"most heartily received"*.

The well-known Naval surname "Garforth" is included in the aforementioned list. The compiler is reminded that, as a young girl in the 1960s, the Misses Garforth (two sisters and descendants) were near-neighbours in St. Leonards. Their brother had been a King's Messenger. The family's strong links with Hastings & St. Leonards are detailed within J.M.Baines's "Historic Hastings" in connection with the visit, in 1873, of Prince Albert Edward of Wales and the younger Prince George, later to become King George V. Staying at the Royal Victoria Hotel, they were particularly taken with the fishing quarter and the Ellen Goodman lifeboat.

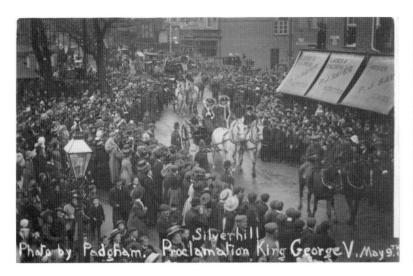

PROCLAMATION OF KING GEORGE V,
9th May 1910.
Morris family members within the throng above - no Radio / Television then!

Above left: Silverhill.
Above right: Queen Victoria "surveys" at Warrior Square, St. Leonards.
Below left: Town Hall, Queen's Road.
Below right: Top of Old Town at incorrectly named "Market Cross".

Above: Coronation Day, 1911.

Left: Bourne Street, Old Town. Fascia board for Watney, Combe, Reid & Co., brewers. Highly decorated hats.
Right: Naval Cadets in procession at White Rock. Bandstand on left in distance.

Below: Hastings Pageant, June 1914. *Left:* Young "swashbucklers" preparing for a Parade.
Right: Watching a sea-plane. The First World War looms.

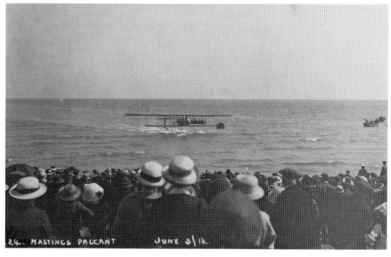

HAPPY TIMES

Left: A very clear, packed beach scene, looking eastwards - Carlisle Parade. Bathing-machines, bathers in sea, all ages on the shingle, Punch and Judy booth in foreground. As they still do today, the Lion and Unicorn, from Buckingham Palace, oversee proceedings opposite Robertson Terrace. Early 1900s.

Below left: Skipping Competition, Children's Fête, August 1908, on "Hastings Sands". Serious expressions on faces of bystanders, stern attendant with badge on jacket, and intense concentration on part of young girl, skipping, with her hair flying.

Below: Preparing for a celebratory parade? - c. 1908. Park Road Methodist Church, corner of Bohemia Road, St. Leonards. Banner reads, "Park Road Wesleyan Band of Hope", (hence children). A very happy day, judging by the facial expressions.

ENTERTAINMENT IN ALEXANDRA PARK, HASTINGS

Above left: Wallis Arthur Concert, 1908. A popular gathering. Youngsters and one elderly gentleman aware of camera - note varied expressions. Early pushchair and perambulators.

Below left: Wallis Arthur's Concert Party, 1916. A very successful impressario, with companies at English resorts for forty years.

Below: Philip William Goepel with his Children's Orchestra about to perform, 5th August 1908. Born in the Old Town, Hastings, in 1869, Goepel died in Rolvenden, Kent, in 1937. A composer of marches and waltzes, he had a mandolin band and led the Red Hungarian Band at local garden parties and balls. Formed his Children's Orchestra for the 1908 Children's Festival in the Park, the instrumentalists comprising about seventy pupils from local Council Schools. According to the Hastings & St. Leonards Observer of 8th August 1908 they were very warmly received, giving an *"altogether praiseworthy performance"*. There is no indication that the Children's Orchestra reformed at any point for other, similar, events.

CENTRAL CRICKET GROUND (PRIORY MEADOW) HASTINGS, AND ARCHERY GARDENS, ST. LEONARDS.

Left: From W. Mate's *Illustrated Guide to Hastings and St. Leonards,* 1900. Dating back to 1864, Priory Meadow was one of the longest established cricket grounds in the country and had links with many famous players. Uniquely situated within the centre of Hastings, it is now the site of a shopping complex. See Page 36 for view of the Ground (originally a medieval harbour) under water.

Above: The Cricket Ground. Photograph by Bradshaw, Hastings.

Right: From W. Mate's *Illustrated Guide to Hastings and St. Leonards,* 1900. Beagley's, who photographed this view, were auctioneers, house, land and estate agents, etc., based in London Road, St. Leonards. (See Page 53 for picture of one of their advertisement hoardings). Here the photographer captures a staged lull during a lawn tennis match (a little girl stands at the side of the net), croquet is being played, and an archery target is visible in the background. Bowls and golf were enjoyed, too. The Guide states "T. R. H. The Duchess of Kent and Princess Victoria founded archery prizes which are annually shot for in these beautiful gardens on the Queen's Birthday by the Royal St. Leonards Archers".

Above: St. Leonards: The Archery Gardens. Photograph by Beagley's, Hastings.

Hastings   Pleasure Yachts.

4353 B.

The Albertine's Crew. Hastings, 1905.

"NEW" ALBERTINE   HASTINGS

PLEASURE YACHTS

These were major beach attractions in the 1890s and early 1900s. Note, *left*, Albertine's crew (and dog), 1905.

WILLIAM SLADE,

Pianoforte and Music Stores,

7, Wellington Place, HASTINGS;

AND

22, Grand Parade, ST. LEONARDS.

SOLE AGENT FOR

STEINWAY,
BECHSTEIN,
WALDEMAR,
THURMER,

AND OTHER CELEBRATED MAKERS.

NEW PIANOFORTES for SALE or HIRE, for a WEEK, MONTH, or YEAR at LOWEST PRICES for CASH.

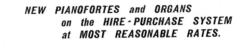

INSPECTION INVITED.

NEW PIANOFORTES and ORGANS on the HIRE-PURCHASE SYSTEM at MOST REASONABLE RATES.

SOLE AGENT FOR

"THE ANGELUS"

Which is a Combination of an Ordinary Pianoforte with an Organ containing Reeds of different qualities of tone.

On this Instrument canbe played the Simplest Melody or the Massive Complicated Symphony.

The most perfect "crescendoes" and "diminuendoes" can be obtained from the faintest "pianissimo" to the loudest "forte" of an Orchestra.

A Large Stock of Second-hand Instruments always on hand.

H. Philpot & Son, The Colonnade, St. Leonards-on-Sea.

ESTABLISHED IN 1836.

A Peaceful Evening at Hastings. *Photo by Godbold.*

MESSRS. PHILPOT & SON have a reputation of over 60 years for the highest standard of Quality and Excellence throughout every department of their business, and in their spacious Showrooms Ladies may be sure of seeing the Latest and Most Exclusive Fashions in every detail of dress at a Moderate Price.

SPECIALTIES :—The Making of **SMART GOWNS, COATS, MANTLES, BLOUSES,** and **MILLINERY** for every occasion by clever and experienced Fitters.

A Stormy Day at St. Leonards. *Photo by Smith.*

Wedding Trousseaux.

Indian Outfits.

Costumes.

Tailor-made Gowns.

Jackets. Mantles.

Laces. Gloves.

Pure Silks.

A Storm at Hastings. *Photo by Godbold.*

Mourning.

Colonial Outfits.

Choice Furs. Millinery.

Lingerie. Blouses and Shirts.

Sunshades and Umbrellas.

Underwear.

Irish Linen and Damasks.

MESSRS. PHILPOT have always on view a very large selection of GOWNS and SKIRTS for Day and Evening Wear and elegant MANTLES and CLOAKS. They are also noted for their FURS and SEALSKINS.

MOURNING ORDERS receive immediate attention and on receipt of letter or wire Experienced Assistants are sent with every requisite.

Reproduced from W. Mate's *Illustrated Guide to Hastings and St. Leonards*, 1900.

STATIONERY AND FANCY GOODS DEPARTMENT.

A LARGE SELECTION OF GOODS ALWAYS IN STOCK, suitable for . . . .

Wedding, Birthday, Christmas, and other Presents,———

Comprising:

Purses, Hand Bags, Cigar and Cigarette Cases, Inkstands, Barometers, Photo Albums, Writing Cases, Glove and Handkerchief Cases, Collar Boxes, Dressing Cases, Jewel Cases, Silver Fruit Knives, Clocks, Electro-Plated and Brass Goods, etc., etc.

CHINA, GLASS, AND BASKET DEPARTMENT.

Die Sinking,———

Relief Stamping,

Printing and Engraving,

AT LOWEST PRICES.

NEWEST DESIGNS IN **Wedding Cards.**

ACCOUNT BOOKS IN ALL RULINGS AND BINDINGS always in Stock.

ALL KINDS NOTE PAPER, ENVELOPES, AND GENERAL STATIONERY.

H. A. Jepson,

(Late BROOKER & JEPSON),

Stationer and Fancy Warehouseman.

SHOW ROOMS:

12, 13, & 14, Robertson Street, HASTINGS.

Depot for "SWAN" FOUNTAIN PENS.

Departments.

STATIONERY, FANCY GOODS, TOYS, GAMES, SPORTS, LEATHER GOODS and TOILET REQUISITES, GLASS and CHINA, CLOCKS and WATCHES, BAGS and TRUNKS, BASKETS and WICKER CABINET GOODS, JAPANESE GOODS, And White Wood for Painting & Poker Work.

TOY DEPARTMENT.

FINE LARGE SHOWROOM FOR TOYS & GAMES of Every Description. ALL NEW GAMES as Published.

Cricket, Tennis, Croquet.

Separate Showroom for BAGS and TRUNKS and all TRAVELLING REQUISITES.

OVERLAND TRUNKS, PATENT CANE TRUNKS, CABIN TRUNKS, GLADSTONE, KIT, BRIEF, and other BAGS.

BAG AND TRUNK DEPARTMENT.

Reproduced from W. Mate's *Illustrated Guide to Hastings and St. Leonards*, 1900.

BOOKS IN STOCK.

FULL DISCOUNT FOR CASH.

3d. in the Shilling.

Purchasers for Libraries, School Prizes, Sunday School Rewards and Presents, will find Selection easy from the Large Stock.

All the Leading Publishers Represented.

A Large Assortment of
CHILDREN'S BOOKS.

Latest Novelties in CALENDERS and BOOKLETS.

FOREIGN : : STAMPS and ALBUMS.

MAGAZINES Supplied.

SPECIAL ORDERS Executed in Two Days.

Parcels from LONDON every Morning.

A Large Stock of
BIBLES, PRAYERS, PRAYER and HYMNS, &c. :

POETS and LEATHER - BOUND BOOKS for Prizes and Presents.

BOOKBINDING.

THEOLOGICAL and DEVOTIONAL WORKS.

ILLUMINATED TEXTS.

GUIDES and CYCLING MAPS.

A. BROOKER,

Late BROOKER and JEPSON,

BOOK SALOON :

16, Robertson Street,

HASTINGS.

Reproduced from W. Mate's *Illustrated Guide to Hastings and St. Leonards*, 1900.

Hunting Breeches.

Ladies' Riding Habits.

Speciality—

Evening Dress.

Walking and Cycling Gowns.

Maconie,

TAILOR,

Robertson St.,

Hastings.

Also at
LONDON AND BEXHILL-ON-SEA.

Corner of Ladies' Fitting Room.

Corner of Gentlemen's Fitting Room.

Reproduced from W. Mate's *Illustrated Guide to Hastings and St. Leonards*, 1900.

BARRANCE & FORD,

_____31, 32 & 33, Robertson, Street, HASTINGS,

And 51A and 51B, KING'S ROAD, BRIGHTON.

Costumes,

Mantles,

Millinery,

Furs,

Parasols,

and

Under=
clothing.

Blouses,

Lace,

Gloves,

Hosiery,

Ribbons,

and all
kinds of

Fancy
Goods.

Separate Showrooms AT
2 and 3, CLAREMONT, HASTINGS,

FOR _Artistic Furniture, Fancy Needlework, Eastern
Merchandise and Art Novelties_ of Every Description.

Reproduced from W. Mate's _Illustrated Guide to Hastings and St. Leonards_, 1900.

In due course, my father's love of books and local history was passed on to me. Like him, I too was an only child, my memories of Hastings and St. Leonards during the 1950s, 1960s and early 1970s as vivid as ever. Rather like a sponge, a child absorbs a great deal and, despite an absence from Sussex from 1977 of nearly 25 years, my memories never faded. Born in 1949, I read a great deal and from a young age was accustomed to being surrounded by my father's ever-burgeoning collection. I am reminded of Eleanor Farjeon's "Author's Note" to *The Little Bookroom* of 1955. She writes, "It would have been more natural to live without clothes than without books. As unnatural not to read as not to eat." This was certainly true in our household. I grew to love the familiar smell and feel of old, and sometimes dusty, volumes, each offering the possibility of some exciting discovery and, in time, a number became firm friends, holding special memories for me. Fanciful though it may sound, a room devoid of books always strikes me as being rather bleak and clinical. (See Pages 20, 23, 65 and 97, plus Appendix on Page 187).

Reading Rider Haggard's exotic tales of adventure, I was highly intrigued to learn that he had lived at North Lodge, Maze Hill, St. Leonards. Then I discovered the evocative writings of Sheila Kaye-Smith, a doctor's daughter, born in Dane Road, not far from Maze Hill. In a book of short stories I came across "Old Gadgett", her poignant tale of an aged Sussex Downland shepherd and his teeth, which led me later to *The Village Doctor* (set in Battle) and then to her atmospheric novel *Tamarisk Town* (published in 1919), this concerning an attempt to develop the fishing village of Marlingate (in reality Hastings) into a fashionable watering-place. One particular favourite was *Picture of Hastings*, from 1826, where I learned about a kangaroo (surely an unusual sight then, and spelled "kanguroo") which travelled, uncomfortably, in a box marked "With Care, This Side Up", by stage-coach from London to Hastings, eating a sandwich en route. What <u>was</u> the creature's fate on arrival? In the same book I read about "a lady in green spectacles" who was desperately upset by the number of bonfires on the beach and by the state of the Fishmarket. Francis Frith's *Gossiping Photographer at Hastings*, from 1864, has particularly good plates, my favourite being the frontispiece (reproduced at the end of the Appendix), showing *St. Mary-in-the-Castle Church* and a highly cluttered beach. Now, burying my nose within its pages, my nostrils still twitch at the familiar smell denoting age and past ownership. *The Story of our Sunday Trip to Hastings*, from 1879, made an impression on me during childhood, this miserable tale detailing the tragic consequences of a Sunday excursion to the town. Inevitably, a copy of Robert Tressell's biting political novel, *The Ragged Trousered Philanthropists*, appeared on a shelf. Originally published in 1914 and set in Mugsborough, i.e. Hastings, the tale concerns working-class life "in the raw" during Edwardian times and became a best-seller. Alongside other Tressell material, including F. C. Ball's *Tressell of Mugsborough*, is a slight volume (one of only 1,500 copies) from 1956, by Frank Swinnerton, entitled *The Adventures of a Manuscript*. This tells the story of how *The Ragged Trousered Philanthropists* came to be published and details F. C. Ball's involvement as Tressell's biographer. In the 1960s a televised adaptation of the novel was shown on BBC 2. (Henry Cousins's books of 1911 and 1920 featured, too).

When I grew older I looked forward to accompanying my father on his dusty, book-buying excursions - sometimes on a Saturday afternoon and frequently during school holidays. Freda Fardoe had a bookshop in Gensing Road, St. Leonards: a niece of Gertrude Lawrence, she was always most welcoming. Elderly (or so he seemed to me) Mr. Walker in Prospect Place concocted a potion to remove "foxing" marks from the pages of books - my father preferred to steer well clear of it. In Claremont was white-haired Mrs. Wilson of *Wilson & Franklin*, the shop eventually changing hands with the arrival of American Stephen Samuelson (who was completely un-American in every way) and his family, whom we came to know well. Just around the corner, in Trinity Street, was *Howes Bookshop* (later at *Trinity Hall* in Braybrooke Terrace) where each side of the staircase was often covered with parcels awaiting despatch - in many cases, I was told, to American universities. Mr. Bowyer would sometimes be in the shop, whereas Raymond Kilgariff, more often than not, was tucked away working on the next catalogue - long before the arrival of modern-day technology. In the heart of the Old Town, at 15 George Street, was the *Powys Bookshop*, where Francis Powys, (of the well-known literary family), who had fought in the Spanish Civil War, always (to my great fascination) nursed a black cat.

At the foot of the High Street, again in the Old Town, was *Floyd's Bookshop*. I can see Mr. Floyd now, sitting in the back of his shop in the gloom of a late Saturday afternoon in winter, surreptitiously reaching for half a pork pie from his desk drawer! He used to tell a good tale which deserves a wider airing. One day a customer entered his shop, wearing a voluminous raincoat, and disappeared behind some bookcases. After a time he emerged, approached Mr. Floyd at his desk, and paid for <u>one</u> item. As he did so, a number of books slid to the floor from underneath his raincoat. Calmly, Mr. Floyd peered at the floor, looked his red-faced customer in the eye, and remarked that he assumed he would be paying for the other items as well? The customer's reaction is not known ..... There were other local booksellers, too, and all of them formed the basis of many enjoyable jaunts, at the end of which, late in the day, we invariably found ourselves at *Kay-Jay's* in Trinity Street where we took the weight off our feet with a pot of tea and hot, buttered toast. *Kay-Jay's* served good, no-nonsense English fare, and the legendary, cheerful "Professor" Percy Press (of national and international *Punch and Judy* fame) always lunched there during the summer season, whereas rascally *Mr. Punch* had other ideas!

Now, looking around my shelves, which house a veritable mixture of volumes including many from my father's collection, yet more bookish memories from childhood return. A number of special Christmas and birthday gifts remind me of those days, such as a lush Bronte set from *Howes Bookshop* and a handsome, leather-bound, illustrated copy of Galsworthy's *Forsyte Saga*, bought from Stephen Samuelson when I reached the age of 21. A slender volume containing A. E. Housman's *A Shropshire Lad* came from Mr. Simmons, a particularly gentlemanly book-dealer whose shop was in Queen's Road. Often, in the late 1960s, I returned home to find Mr. Simmons on the point of leaving, having enjoyed an afternoon with my father discussing books. Upon his death, very generously he left the bulk of his estate (settled by my father as executor) for the benefit of the elderly of the town, through the *Blackman Foundation*. In the 21st century, book-dealing has changed beyond all recognition and, very largely, the personal touch has disappeared, possibly due to the arrival of the Internet. Arnold Bennett's bookselling novel *Riceyman Steps*, from 1923, comes to mind, as I remember reading the paperback edition during the mid-1960s.

As a child I was introduced by my father to *Hastings Museum* at John's Place and to *The Old Town Hall Museum* in the High Street, my favourite exhibit being a nineteenth century, telescopic, panoramic "Peepshow" depicting the sea-front. I remember the excellent rapport John Manwaring Baines, the then Curator, enjoyed with youngsters such as me. Probably in 1971, in the company of my father, I attended one of Mr. Baines's talks, this being on the subject of the *Amsterdam*, the Dutch East Indiaman beached near Bulverhythe. Surprisingly, not many were present, but interesting items from the wreck were on display, mainly bottles. I have known *The Fishermen's Museum* for years, too, and remember buying a 1964 calendar, showing the *Enterprise* lugger, this being the main internal display since 1956. I still have it, tucked away. Now, when I look up at the walls, crammed with local names and exhibits, many different memories come flooding back - some happy, some sad. As I gaze at the albatross in its display case, I am whisked back to Hastings of the late 1960s and to the happy day in 1968 when, from a shop in Castle Street, I bought the record *Albatross* by the "pop" group *Fleetwood Mac*. In its "modern" instrumental way, it is so evocative of the sea. A sad memory of that time concerns the horrific Hither Green railway disaster. On Sunday 5th November 1967, the twelve-coach 7:43 p.m. diesel-electric Hastings to Charing Cross train was literally overflowing with passengers, many of them being forced to stand in the corridors. The train was travelling from Orpington and was approaching Hither Green at about 70 mph when a broken rail caused a severe derailment. Forty-nine passengers were killed and seventy-eight were injured (twenty-seven seriously). Many were young people travelling back to London to study or to work, having visited relatives in East Sussex. The population being smaller then than now, everyone seemed to be affected in some way or other. Two of my schoolfriends each lost a brother on that fateful night.

Inevitably, my earliest memories of Hastings focus on the sea and swimming. I learned to swim (like so many other children) with the help of Mr. Ryper at Hastings Baths on the sea-front. I can still conjure up the taste and smell of the chlorinated sea-water, along with the warm, damp atmosphere, the Victorian Baths being fully enclosed. I remember 2nd August 1959, the day on which I swam 55 yards, using the breast-stroke, and how proud I was to receive my certificate - which I still have! However, I much preferred splashing in the open air, so I always looked forward to visiting the huge Bathing Pool (long-gone) at West Marina, St. Leonards, built to Olympic specifications in 1933. (See Pages 80 and 91).

I loved the beach, too. I recall the feel of the shingle under my bare feet and the "pulling" sensation of the undertow when paddling, not to mention the glorious, salty taste on the lips, along with the familiar, briny smell pungently assailing my nostrils. I came to know and love the sea in all its many moods. Never to be forgotten was the distinctive "raking" sound caused by the undertow dragging at the shingle - a sure sign of bad weather to come. Sometimes the temperature dropped dramatically as a cool, clammy, all-enveloping mist (a "fret") rolled in from the sea. I remember delicious ice-cream being sold on Hastings beach. The ice-cream seller had a well-stocked "cool-box" slung around his neck (rather reminiscent of that carried by a cinema usherette), but his supply was soon depleted as he tramped over the shingle. He then left the beach, returning shortly with further supplies. As a treat, I was sometimes taken to *The Creamery*, in Robertson Street, often being defeated by gargantuan ice-cream sundaes. Early in the morning, if the tide was out, I noticed much frantic activity as people dug for lugworm, and at night nothing compared with looking out to sea, with all lights switched off and a bright moon shining down. (See Pages 83 and 87).

The weather was not always kind, though. I recall the full fury of gale-force winds from the Channel, accompanied by lashing rain which stung my cheeks as I tried to keep my balance when struggling along the sea-front. In the days before mobile 'phones and pagers, the lifeboat maroon was often heard, signalling that someone was in trouble. (See Page 79). The vicious winter of 1962-63 was particularly memorable: snow started to fall on Boxing Day, with the weather worsening rapidly thereafter. Roads and pavements became treacherous, with underground drains freezing in Hastings and water supplies to certain homes being affected. There was to be no relief from the Arctic conditions for about three months.

During my childhood, there was always plenty of entertainment in Hastings to be enjoyed. Many happy times were spent at the *White Rock Pavilion* (now *Theatre*) and I took part every Spring from about the age of seven in the annual *Hastings Musical Festival*, particularly remembering the friendly rivalry (when older) surrounding the award of the *John Lockey Banner* for school choral-singing. In 1956 the *White Rock* staged an exhibition featuring material by local artists who contributed works which were sold in aid of victims of the Hungarian Uprising. My mother and I eventually staggered home with three flower paintings, one of which was by Muriel Jackson who lived in Croft Road. In that same year I saw my first *Hastleon* production at the *White Rock*, this being *Song of Norway* (concerning the composer Grieg) which was followed by many other hugely entertaining and lavish spectacles such as *My Fair Lady* and *South Pacific*. In 1959 *The Yeomen of the Guard* was staged. I was amongst a party of excited children helping to celebrate a schoolfriend's birthday and we were seated in the front row of the Circle. As expected, the performance was well-attended and, looking down, I managed to pick out my parents in the Stalls, my mother being particularly fond of Gilbert & Sullivan. The *Hastleons* (amateurs and still flourishing) were formed in 1925, the name (half Hastings, half St. Leonards) representing a group of energetic individuals, such as John Woodhams of *Brufords*, Eastbourne, and Tom Wood (by day to be found at the Head Office of the *Hastings & East Sussex Building Society*), dedicated to the production of musicals, all well supported. (See Pages 82 and 190).

There was just one "blip", though. In the 1960s there were relatively few overseas students in the town. My Thai friends, whom I knew very well indeed (one living with us for a while due to accommodation problems) were bitterly upset by the 1966 staging of the musical *The King & I*. They revered their Royal Family and did not approve of such a frivolous production, even considering parts of it to be sacrilegious. (Through Maliwan Isaryakunakorn, I was introduced to smokily flavoured *Lapsang Souchong* tea and authentic Far-Eastern dishes). I have particularly fond memories, from the 1950s, of the famed *NALGO* Christmas pantomimes with Reg Taylor playing the part of the Dame - exuberantly, to say the least. They were splendidly boisterous shows and we youngsters were actively encouraged to let our hair down. Those of us "in the know" realised that, if we delayed our departure following a performance, we would be rewarded by the Dame, and others in the cast, emerging from behind the scenes and visiting us personally in the body of the *Pavilion*. In effect, we would be treated to an "extra" show, always well received! A visit to the *NALGO* pantomime signified that Christmas-time was fast approaching, and I returned home afterwards to start making up lots of festive paper-chains as my contribution to the celebrations.

During the 1950s, Cyril Fletcher's *White Rock* summer shows, in which he starred with his wife, Betty Astell, generated much fun. Providing lively entertainment, they included lots of song-and-dance routines with plenty of colourful costumes and sets. It is impossible to forget the comedian's "Odd Odes". Following his being made a member of the well-known *Hastings Winkle Club* (formed in 1900 by the fishermen of the Old Town to help the less fortunate, and still going strong today), Cyril Fletcher penned the lines shown on Page 88, these being reproduced from *Winkle Up!*, by "Bill" Dyer and "Bill" Vint, published in 1972.

In time I visited *The Stables Theatre* which, prior to restoration and conversion in 1958, had suffered a chequered past, originally being Georgian stabling dating from 1746. Later, horses attached to the Duke of Wellington's troops were stabled there. I remember accompanying a friend to a production of *Othello* which I found, I am sorry to say, rather gruelling. Much more to my taste was a lively, colourful production one Christmas (probably in 1971) of the old favourite *A Christmas Carol* by Charles Dickens. I recall the festive, happy atmosphere when everyone spilled out afterwards into the cold night air of the Old Town. (See Page 79).

In the summer I enjoyed energetic trips on the *Old Town Boating Lake*. In those days the boats were realistically designed, having thick, rubber bumpers which acted as protection in the event of a not infrequent collision. I loved breezy kite-flying, too, my father and I using the East and West Hill Lifts to obtain the full benefit of the wind, plus marvellous views. A particularly strong memory is of watching (and hearing!) the colourfully-dressed Town Criers from all over the country who competed regularly in the U. K. Championships held every summer in Hastings: an extremely popular event when staged on the Pier. Huge crowds milled about nearby, listening to the familiar and raucous bellow "Oyez! Oyez!" carried in their direction by the wind. Thankfully, the Hastings Crier was not expected to demonstrate one of his long-vanished duties, that of whipping criminals of both sexes, in the 18th century receiving one shilling for each unfortunate miscreant who came his way. On the Pier itself were rows of neatly-arranged deck-chairs, and I remember sitting in one under the merciless, baking-hot sun. In the late 1950s, frequent trips by Paddle Steamer were enjoyed, embarking from the end of Hastings Pier, and I can still recall the exciting, throbbing sensation under my feet as we set out. Never to be forgotten were the outings to the *Royal Sovereign Lightship*. Strong arms were needed as we hurled bundles of magazines across to the men on duty! A point worthy of note is that Hastings Pier, in the 1960s, played host to all the major "pop" groups of the day, including *The Rolling Stones*, with just one strange exception - *The Beatles*. (See Pages 81, 82, 85 and 93).

When I was young there were many cinemas in the area. My first outing to *The Gaiety* in Queen's Road was in the 1950s with my mother to see *Around the World in Eighty Days*, starring David Niven as Jules Verne's character, Phineas Fogg. In the 1960s, at the same cinema, I saw *The Beatles* in *A Hard Day's Night*, a schoolfriend and I going to an afternoon showing during the summer holidays: oddly, in view of the hysteria surrounding the group, the attendance was very small. This cinema had an excellent cafe where afternoon tea could be enjoyed. *The Curzon*, in Norman Road, St. Leonards, was another favourite haunt where I saw lavish films such as *Breakfast at Tiffany's* and *Thoroughly Modern Millie*. Melancholic Tony Hancock appeared in *The Punch and Judy Man* which I remember seeing at *The Orion*, sited close to the (much missed since 1973) *Albert Memorial* in Hastings Town Centre. Fondly referred to as the local "flea-pit", with seats sagging almost to the floor, *The Orion* served up other delights, too, such as *Cleopatra*. In Cambridge Road was *The Ritz (ABC)* which became a Sainsbury's supermarket and then a Co-op store.

On a quieter note, *Alexandra Park* could be relied upon for good walks, and *Linton Gardens* for seclusion. The area within *St. Leonards Gardens* devoted to plants grown specifically with the blind in mind, all being chosen carefully for their different scents and textures, made a strong impression on me. Meanwhile, *White Rock Gardens*, with its outstanding views, housed the Tudor-style *Model Village*, perfect for a small child. Sometimes I was taken into *St. Mary-in-the-Castle Church* (long before it became an Arts Centre) where I was puzzled by the water trickling out of the rock and I wondered at the depth of the Immersion Font. Dating from 1828, the building has outstanding acoustics and, as already mentioned, was where my father's maternal grandparents were married. (See Page 92 for *Model Village* detail).

Fifty years ago, shopping for food (and its storage) was handled very differently from today. There were many individual shops in the Hastings area, owned and/or staffed by people keenly interested in promoting their businesses and willing to provide customers with personal attention. Naturally this included a home-delivery service, if required, even on small orders. There were no domestic freezers such as now, the refrigerators of that time having small inbuilt "freezing" compartments capable of holding not much more than a packet of frozen peas and a block of ice-cream. Additionally, the kitchen would have a cool larder in which to store other foodstuffs, including tinned and bottled items. As a result, perishable foods had to be bought frequently and in relatively small quantities. There were no "convenience foods" or "fast-food" outlets (save for fish-and-chip shops) and meals had to be cooked from scratch, using basic ingredients, plus salads, fruits and vegetables which were in season. Now, more often than not, everything is bought in one visit from an anonymous supermarket with produce (frequently exotic) being available all year round, from all parts of the globe, largely as a result of ease of air transport. Internet shopping is an impersonal experience.

Similarly, the eating habits of half a century ago were enormously different, largely because children (and adults) led far more physically active lives than today. Children walked to and from school, using public transport only if travelling a distance or if the weather was bad. Others cycled - there was relatively little traffic on the roads - and children were not ferried about as they are today. In addition, youngsters needed a lot of "inner fuel" as, unlike now, there was frequently much sporting activity to be enjoyed or endured during the day. As a result, I always had a cooked breakfast, plus a milky drink, a practice then widely advocated, but frowned upon today as the vast majority lead more sedentary lives. Milk was delivered as a matter of course every day, excluding Sunday, and I well remember *Fagg & Son*, greengrocers, next door to *Lovibond*, grocers, in King's Road, St. Leonards. For grocery, *Cave-Austin* at Grand Parade, and at Marina, could be relied upon, too. There was far less pre-packaging, with bacon (green or smoked) being sliced, as a matter of course, to the exact thickness required by the customer (no shiny, wet, packaged rashers then), and huge cheeses of various types were divided up according to the customer's wishes, finally being wrapped in greaseproof paper. Vegetables were never pre-washed so that celery, for example, unlike now, was always filthy dirty, being covered in soot and properly blanched. Once cleaned up, using a tooth-brush kept specially for the purpose, it was beautifully white and crisp, with a delicious nutty flavour. The name of Arthur Fagg was well-known in cricketing circles and his daughter had married Mr. Hender, a close schoolfriend of the comedian Tommy Trinder - Mr. and Mrs. Hender together ran the King's Road shop. Also in King's Road was cheerful Mrs. Turk of *The Smoke Room*, selling cigarettes and tobacco (now, I suppose, politically incorrect). I remember furniture sometimes being bought from evocatively-named *Elijah Gray* of London Road, St. Leonards. *Adams & Jarrett* (for electrical goods) in Norman Road and *Gordon Busbridge* (for furniture, established in the early 1900s) have, happily, expanded considerably since my day.

Mr. Beresford "Bill" Beck, the well-known St. Leonards baker, deserves a paragraph in his own right. I shall never forget him - a wonderful character, a great mimic, and an expert on the inner workings of clocks and watches. His bread was delicious, too! For a number of years we were indeed lucky to have Mr. Beck's bread, delivered personally by him several times a week, he being based at his family's long-established business in East Ascent, St. Leonards. Opened there by Mr. Beck's great-grandfather in 1832, a wood-fired oven had been used to bake bread for Princess Victoria when she stayed in St. Leonards as a girl. Each Good Friday during Victorian times was marked by the Beck family throwing Hot Cross Buns out to hordes of expectant children waiting excitedly in the street. Even when we moved into Hastings from St. Leonards, thankfully Mr. Beck (and his ancient van) followed us. However, this happy state of affairs was not destined to last. It was a sad day when he was forced, through no fault of his own, to close down - due to ridiculous, pettifogging regulations. All his work surfaces were of wood and this, apparently, was not good enough for the authorities who insisted he must change over to "modern, man-made" surfaces instead. Mr. Beck's current, solid brick, coal-fired oven, installed in 1860, did not pass muster, apparently, and the upshot was predictable: the business closed in 1972. Before the introduction of modern winding mechanisms, Mr. Beck was the last in a line of men who climbed the 66 steps to wind the clock at *Christ Church*, St. Leonards, performing this task three times a week: according to him, 237 turns were needed for each day! He also found "time" to wind the clock at *St. John's Church*. (See Pages 94 and 95).

Wonderful afternoon teas (with luscious fresh cream eclairs) were enjoyed upstairs, overlooking the sea, at *Addison's*, the long-established and sadly-missed caterers and pastry-cooks at Marina, St. Leonards. For general sale they produced delectable cakes and other treats, too, such as pork and asparagus rolls, for which customers travelled miles. Continental confectionery items, such as *Droste* chocolate, were stocked as a matter of course at a time, half a century ago, when this was quite unusual in our area. One day I received a gift of a fanciful pale-pink plastic fish, containing tiny sweets, fashioned to resemble small pebbles. I kept the fish, proving this had been a good choice of present for a youngster. A postcard from grandmother's album shows the *East Sussex Hospital Cake* of 1912, pictured on Page 5, and is a fine example of *Addison's* skills. Beautifully decorated, it features items of local interest including fishing-boats ('RX' to the fore), and summer pastimes such as cricket, cycling and croquet. I remember the last member of the Addison family - he always looked so pale, perhaps due to the heat of the kitchens. Much earlier in the 20th century, *Semadeni*, of No. 6, Claremont, were in a similar line of business. Celebrated French and Swiss pastrycooks and established in the late 1870s, they sold teas, coffees and ices, but they were especially noted for their exquisite, hand-made confectionery. When my father was a young man and visiting his aunts, no homecoming was complete without the gift of a mouth-watering selection of chocolates or creams from *Semadeni!*

Just along from *Addison's* was *Philpot's* - established 1836, and closed 1986. They were drapers, ladies' hairdressers and stockists of ladies' fashions. Passing over the threshold was a case of stepping back in time to a much gentler, more leisurely age. I can still picture, on the ground floor, the delicate early-Victorian chairs which were positioned by various counters for the use of customers. Ladies' hairdressing needs were attended to (and absolute privacy assured) by the provision of individual cubicles - there was nothing so undignified as an open-plan salon! Upstairs, where I recall outerwear being purchased, was lush carpeting along with sofas by the windows overlooking the sea, and always an aura of overwhelming calm ..... When I was quite young, I was sent one morning to *Philpot's* with a message for Miss Perch on the gloves counter. I was most surprised to be told, "Miss Perch is at lunch", but learned later that this was an old, Sussex, reference to "elevenses". Strictly speaking, the term covers any meal not eaten at a table. In the late 1960s I received a present of a full-length summery "lounger" with three-quarter sleeves, mandarin collar and zipped front, this coming from *Philpot's*. Made from delicate cotton, the design was typical of the era, involving psychedelic swirls of mainly sea-green and blue. As expected, it did not have any sewn-in washing instructions bearing the now ubiquitous "symbols", as these did not appear until the 1970s.

Within the centre of Hastings, long before the sad disappearance of the *Albert Memorial* and the Cricket Ground, and prior to pedestrianisation and new road lay-outs, were many excellent shops, particularly in bustling Robertson Street, home of *The Creamery*, previously mentioned. One such was *Plummer Roddis*, a department store (known as *Plummer's*, now *Debenhams*). Here, in the late 1960s, I bought a paper dress from a good selection. This was the time of the "Swinging Sixties", and the idea of a paper dress was quite novel. It was supposedly washable, but despite the fact that the "material" was reasonably tough, disappointingly it had to be disposed of after a short while! *Plummer's* later introduced a useful delicatessen counter within the store. (See Page 84).

Madame Greenaway supplied lingerie and swimwear, as well as much unhurried personal attention and advice regarding the fitting of corsetry. *George H. Hall*, (which became *Jones*), established in 1855, was excellent for footwear, with the redoubtable Miss Nicholson in charge. She kept a stern eye on proceedings. As a child, I used the "X-ray machine" sited at the back of the shop, this being an aid to sizing. Once a customer was happy with a pair of shoes, the assistant <u>always</u> summoned Miss Nicholson from the rear of the premises to check that the shoes fitted correctly. Finally, the customer was <u>always</u> escorted to the door which was <u>always</u> held open by the assistant. Needless to say, it was <u>never</u> necessary to ask for a shoe-horn! There was a separate area for gentlemen's shoes, under the care of Mr. Hardy, and all repairs were carried out subterraneously, a spiral staircase leading down to the nether regions in a way rather reminiscent of the film *Hobson's Choice*, starring Charles Laughton and John Mills.

Jepson's was another shop which must not be overlooked. With the super-efficient Miss Power in charge, it stocked all manner of pens, stationery, wools, small leather articles and many unusual items. Grandmother had known the shop since very early girlhood and insisted upon a special excursion there every Christmas to purchase small gifts. In the late 1950s *Jepson's* advertised thus within the pages of *Kelly's Directory*: "Our Toy Showrooms are the largest on the South Coast". I still use a large, sturdy, brown leather bag bought from *Jepson's* and I recall Miss Power remarking sagely: "That bag will see you out, Miss Scrivens", and I think she will be proved right.

In Claremont, (and also at Marina, St. Leonards) was Mr. Mitchell for greengrocery, plus Mr. Salmon, the chemist (previously *Bolshaw*) from whom it was always possible to buy something special for, say, a birthday or at Christmas-time, as well as *Farmers' Direct Dairies*. Mr. Wilshin (five times Mayor of Hastings in the 1960s), of 3 Claremont (formerly of Queen's Road) ran a ladies' outfitters and hosiery business. He was always helpful and cheerful whenever I called into the shop, to collect, say, a new supply of tights - life was less fraught then. There was terrific excitement at the changeover to these from stockings in the 1960s - necessary in the days of very short skirts. This era saw much social change, including the start of a gradual relaxation of the previously, generally accepted, formal "dress-code". From 1971 onwards we came to know helpful Mrs. Cole and Mr. Kilbey very well indeed - based close to Claremont Steps they sold confectionery and tobacco, enjoying a bustling trade.

At White Rock was Mr. Goldup of *Arthur Green* (the gentlemen's outfitters), whom my father had known since early adulthood. Back in the mid-1920s, Aunt Harriet had treated her young nephew to a new raincoat, taking him into *Arthur Green* for the first time. Latterly, Mr. Goldup was cheerfully assisted by Mr. Hunt, who was in his eighties. Here in the 1960s I bought oversize sweaters, "Sloppy Joe" jumpers being all the rage - and *Arthur Green* had an excellent range, but not originally intended for young girls! *Salmon's*, again in White Rock, and still trading, took care of stationery needs and new book requirements, also providing a useful Post Office service. *Cherry Brothers* in Robertson Street had cooked meats; round in Queen's Road was Mr. Hickman, the butcher; and in Cambridge Gardens was Mr. Anderson, grocer, who specialised in cooking his own succulent hams. For ironmongery needs, Mr. Mozley (whose daughter, Jennifer, was in my class at the *Mary Wray Secretarial College*) could be found in York Buildings, his business latterly badly-hit by D. I. Y. stores.

Two particularly strong memories remain with me from the 1950s. The first is of *Sainsbury's*, in Wellington Place, which sold delicious, smoked, pork sausages. When cooked, these developed a most mouthwatering crisp skin, the taste of which I can still conjure up. Those were the days long before *Sainsbury's* became a massive, impersonal supermarket chain, and I recall the assistants weighing out and patting up butter to a customer's individual requirements, using wooden butter-pats. Secondly, I remember accompanying my mother to *Mastin's* (established 1872, closed 1969) in Castle Street and in Breeds Place. This was a drapers, milliners and soft furnishings store, and also stocked ladies' fashions. I particularly remember the contraption known as the "overhead railway" which was brought into play when we came to pay for our purchases. Payment was tucked inside a metal cylinder, with the account, and, by a series of pulleys, despatched across the ceiling to the Cash Desk where the contents were dealt with. Any change, and the receipted account, would be returned to the customer by the same method. (See Page 85).

There were many other such shops, but those I have detailed give an indication as to the variety available some fifty years ago. In those days shopping was a happy experience, not the soulless chore of today. A particular favourite of mine, as a child, was the *Mary Rushbrooke Studio* in the High Street, Old Town. Here, in the double-fronted windows, I could rely on finding an incredible display of ceramic figures, fascinating to any youngster: clowns, jesters, and assorted animals such as mice would greet me as I passed by. I was lucky enough to be given one, which I still have.

When I was growing up, it was accepted that clothing <u>lasted.</u> Shoes were mended, socks were darned (haberdashers are elusive now) and domestic items (umbrellas included) were repaired locally if they broke. Now we live in an age of seemingly planned obsolescence - truly a throwaway society, drowning under unnecessary packaging. There has been another significant social change, too, which has occurred over the last forty years. Some readers may be surprised by my references to <u>surnames</u> rather than <u>first</u> names. As a youngster, I <u>never</u> addressed my elders by their first names. Nowadays, virtually everywhere, the usage of first names in conversation is taken for granted from the moment of introduction. This was certainly not so when I was a child. Adults addressed each other by surname, too, (unless, of course, speaking to family members). Formality (as with clothing) was very much the order of the day, and it took a long time indeed to become on first-name terms. From my earliest days when working, I was always called, by my elders, "Miss Scrivens" (never "Cynthia"). It was the accepted way then. I suppose this practice continued until the early 1970s, by which stage I became aware of the onset of a more free-and-easy attitude within the workplace. Perhaps this subtle change occurred earlier in centres of population bigger than Hastings.

In 1962, when just thirteen years old, I was taken by my father to lunch at the much-missed *Castle Hotel* in Wellington Square, Hastings. Opened originally in 1818, I remember its Regency style well and my surroundings impressed me enormously. There was a lot of crisp white napery and, it being a warm, summer's day, the sun was streaming through the wide-open windows. I was presented with an enormous Dover Sole which, somehow, I managed to handle with aplomb! (See Page 89).

Wellington Square was developed prior to 1824. At No. 43 could be found the small, and independently run, *Mary Wray Secretarial College*, at which, in January 1967, I began a course of good, old-fashioned secretarial training under the watchful eye of the then principal, Mr. H. S. Upton. The *College* (long-gone) had a first-class reputation, and obtained consistently good results in public examinations. In the late 1960s, Mary Wray, a highly-skilled shorthand-writer, was still "in residence", together with her husband Kenneth Wray, who ran his architect's practice from the same address.

Mr. Upton was a top-class teacher of *Pitman's* shorthand: in truth, one of the best teachers I have known. Once the basic shorthand skills had been acquired, every Friday afternoon was devoted to the furtherance of our "speeds". Along one wall of the classroom was a large board covered with pins, each one indicating a student's progress, week by week. Standing in front of the class, and behind a lectern, Mr. Upton (stop-watch in hand) always had a large glass of water close by - an essential aid on a Friday afternoon. A neat pile of previously selected dictation exercises lay before him (company reports and accounts being particular favourites) and a different item was selected for each speed. Starting at 50 words per minute (w.p.m.), eventually he would be speaking at 120/130/140 w.p.m., inevitably becoming extremely red-faced through sheer exertion. Perhaps it was as well he had the weekend in which to recover!

Typewriting was taught by Mrs. Upton. I can still picture the typing room which, in the days long before word-processors and computers, must have contained over 20 models of manual typewriter (*Adler; Olivetti, Olympia, Remington, Royal,.....*) each one of which we had to use, in order to become familiar with them all. Changing a ribbon often resulted in grubby fingers and thumbs, and typing on a manual machine was hard, laborious, physical work. A lot of attention was paid to the English language in general and spelling in particular. One topic which occupied a fair amount of time concerned the splitting of words at the end of lines so that a satisfactory right-hand margin could be achieved - a skill not needed with present-day technology! When typing, great care had to be taken not to make errors as the correction of these was time-consuming and messy, involving the use of a typewriter eraser (rather like a toughened pencil-rubber) and protective pieces of paper. In those days there was no way of making an amendment "invisibly". We spent much time being taught how to display complicated material accurately, using arithmetical calculations, and woe betide us if we had difficulty, for this formed an important part of the examination syllabus. Pocket calculators were not common then.

General office practice (as it was in the 1960s) featured strongly on the curriculum, too, covering delights such as the cutting of stencils, duplicating, various filing systems, petty cash, postage book, telegrams, the handling of correspondence, etc. Re-reading Mr. Upton's dictated notes, after more than forty years, I hear again his measured and precise tones:

"Remember, the stencil is the medium through which hundreds or thousands of copies will be produced. Every flaw in the preparation will be reproduced on each copy - see there are no flaws. Arrange to display the work artistically. There should be no difficulty here as each stencil is printed with scales to help in the arrangement ......"

Youngsters may be surprised by the seemingly antiquated procedures described, but I am certain I will have jogged the memories of older readers. The great strides in office technology, now taken for granted, such as the arrival of word-processors, computers, pocket calculators, Fax machines, and of course the Internet, have come about only in recent years. Electric typewriters were then in their infancy: one such lived in the office and each of us had to spend several days, during our final term, becoming accustomed to its strange ways.

Mr. Upton was a strict disciplinarian, standing no nonsense. On my first day, to my great surprise, I met up with a friend not seen for seven years. During our mid-morning break, she and I, together with another student, decamped to *Lyons* cafe in nearby Wellington Place. There we chatted and enjoyed our coffee, failing to keep a close enough eye on the clock. We were five minutes late in returning and there, waiting on the stairs for us, pocket-watch in hand, stood Mr. Upton. Glaring at us, he remarked coldly, "This is a fine way to start your time here, is it not?", and continued by making it abundantly clear that he would not tolerate any further examples of lax time-keeping. His was a stern regime, but none the worse for that. In the event, and after this inauspicious start, I was very happy at No. 43 Wellington Square, learning much from Mr. and Mrs. Upton. I kept in touch long after marriage and leaving Hastings, exchanging news on a regular basis. There have been considerable changes in the way of secretarial tuition and office technology, but nothing will ever replace *Pitman's* shorthand as it is an infallible system. In later years, I realised its true worth as I was frequently in London, taking minutes of meetings at which forty or more attendees (many with strong regional accents) often spoke heatedly and at speed.

My first term at *Mary Wray's* was marred by a bout of measles: lying in a darkened room for two weeks I got behind with my studies and, frustratingly, missed two episodes of the first showing of the original, highly-acclaimed black-and-white BBC adaptation of Galsworthy's *Forsyte Saga*, which took the country (Hastings included) by storm. There were no video recorders then!

In our final term, each student had a week's work experience at a different local firm. Mine was at the Head Office of the *Hastings & East Sussex Building Society* (another small concern, sadly long-vanished) of 13 Wellington Place, later my first employer. This proved to be a strange quirk of fate as I had grown up with the old Building Society movement. In 1931 my father joined the *Halifax Building Society* (with its then, and for many years, strong Victorian benevolent and philanthropic ideals, always describing himself as "a Building Society man". He keenly advocated the principle of mutuality, sadly abandoned by the *Halifax* some years ago in favour of becoming a public limited company. During my secretarial course I decided I should buy myself a portable, manual typewriter with which to practise typing at home, so in 1967 I visited *Beechings* (office equipment suppliers) in Havelock Road, coming away with a little *Olympia*.

I was fortunate in that the *Hastings & East Sussex Building Society* was my first employer back in 1968. Founded in 1851, there were branches in St. Leonards, Bexhill, Battle, Maidstone, Ashford, Tenterden and Folkestone. The *Hastings & East Sussex* was paternalistic, in keeping with old

Building Society tradition, and I absorbed a great deal, being in the "outside world", so to speak, for the first time. At the Head Office in Hastings, I worked in a long upstairs room overlooking the hustle and bustle of Wellington Place (many years before pedestrianisation), being situated conveniently close to *Lloyds Bank*, "descendants" of the *Hastings Old Bank*. Sitting behind my trusty full-size *Olympia* typewriter, I dealt with mortgage arrears and insurance matters in my early days, helping out on mortgage applications as required. When taken to task about my lack of speed, regarding the production of these papers, I pointed out that I was taking care to centre everything <u>precisely</u> - doing arithmetical calculations as taught at *Mary Wray's*. How I was shrieked at! "Get a move on! You're not taking exams now! Judge it by eye!" And, as instructed, I <u>did</u> get a move on! My hours, Monday to Friday, were 9:00 a.m. to 5:00 p.m., with 1½ hours for lunch (this seeming particularly generous) and Saturday mornings were worked on a rota system. Some of the surnames from those times come flooding back: Addison, Bond, Coote, Cruttenden, Jukes, Mabbett, Maguire, Morley, Murphy, Ransom, Rich, Wheeler, Wren,..... (See Page 92).

I will always remember the *Mary Wray Secretarial College* and the *Hastings & East Sussex Building Society* with much affection as each, in its own way, provided solid "grounding" which stood me in good stead for the future. My childhood was drawing to a close and I suppose it was highly fitting that it ended with my happy 21st birthday celebration, in 1970, at the *Coach House Restaurant* in All Saints Street where - yes! - I enjoyed grilled Dover Sole in the company of my father - just as I had done in 1962 at the *Castle Hotel*.

Even today, I recall the curious Sussex expressions used, as a matter of course, by my father and paternal grandmother. Both steadfastly refused to be "druv", being by nature fiercely independent. If grandmother sought my father's opinion, she invariably received a reply along the following lines: "Why ask me? I'll tell you what I think, but it won't make any difference because you've already decided what to do, anyway!" The "raking" sound of the sea at certain times has been covered and I have mentioned the familiar "sea-fret", too. Due to the all-pervading nature of this mist, even in the height of summer it sometimes seemed as if Hastings had skipped several months and we were in the middle of November. Great-grandfather always referred to his walking-stick as his "bat", never using the word "stick". This was an accepted term locally, but when my father, as a very small boy, was first asked to fetch the "bat", this request puzzled him enormously. Even when elderly, my father referred to sheep as "ship", hence the saying, "Spoiling the ship for a ha'p'orth of tar". This relates to Sussex sheep-shearers and the tar-boy who applied tar to any snicks or cuts in order to prevent the "ship" attracting further trouble from, say, flies. A heron would be called "Jack-earn", a muddly head was described as "swimy" and someone straightforward and staunch would be known as "jonnick", this last being a particular favourite of his. Narrow alleyways were always "twittens" and travelling pedlars were known as "higglers", from which comes today's expression "higgledy-piggledy". As a youngster, my father had been ill with "glass-pox", and he was unsure as to whether this was an old Sussex expression for, say, chicken-pox, measles, or German measles, but I think it is probable that it was one of these so-called "childhood diseases". Maybe, or even "mayhap", someone will be able to throw light on this term. With relatives and friends in the outlying country areas, local place-names were often conveniently shortened, so that Bodiam, Burwash, Heathfield and Sedlescombe became respectively "Bodjum", "Berrish", "Heffle" and "Selscum".

With hindsight (a "wunnerful" thing) I wish I had asked more of my father and grandmother about the past. When not elsewhere, my grandparents lived in Boreham Street at *Kia Ora* (Maori for "Good Health"), Bertie Morris having emigrated to New Zealand in 1908. Following Tom's death in 1942, Alice remained at the same address with her sister, Annie, who died in 1956, Alice dying in 1969. Having a number of relatives nearby, both sisters had known the area since childhood. I remember many visits, the house containing all manner of curiosities handed down from previous generations. As a youngster, my favourites were two Victorian cast-iron doorstops fashioned in the form of the Duke of Wellington and The Lion. Originally belonging to great-grandmother in Hastings during the 1860s, but perhaps slightly older, they were never separated and, at 16 inches tall, stood guard in grandmother's Boreham Street hallway. I suppose they made such an impression on me because, when I first knew them, I was about the same height. They are still on duty, but with me.

I found the garden (in those days secluded in many places and open in others) fascinating, with soft fruits and vegetables being cultivated, too. In the orchard different types of apple were grown, including *Beauty of Bath* which had to be picked at just the right time before going woolly in texture. Subsequent owners razed the orchard to the ground which meant the permanent loss of many old varieties of apple (previously always carefully stored over the winter), choosing instead to install donkeys.

I recall as a small child (during the very early 1950s) sleeping at my grandmother's house, and can bring to mind the almost overpowering silence of the surrounding countryside at night. As I lay in bed, sometimes the stillness would be shattered by the sound of a solitary motor-bike, coming ever nearer, nearer..... only to fade away, gradually, in the distance, whereupon the eerie, all enveloping silence would descend once more. I later discovered that the culprit responsible for disturbing the peace was an Automobile Association patrolman who lived locally and was returning home.

In Victorian and Edwardian times, Boreham Street was very self-contained (unlike now) having everything necessary for day-to-day living close at hand, at a time when travel was dependent on the horse. The long-established Village Stores and Post Office (both of which were personally and closely linked to members of grandmother's family) provided all daily requirements, and more besides, remembering, too, that the farms in the neighbourhood employed much labour, unlike now, an age of almost complete mechanisation. *Windmill Hill Place*, for some years a well-known Lawn Tennis Centre, used to be the home of the Curteis family (who were related to the Ashburnhams) and in their day regular deliveries were made by the Village Stores. Sweets, chocolate, tobacco, grocery, greengrocery, haberdashery, ironmongery, household linens, cookery-ware, crockery, hip-baths, ewers and bowls, buckets, ... you name it, it was stocked: photographs and the inventory from 1873 show the importance of the enterprise. The premises are now occupied by *Scolfe's Tearooms*, the structure being a Grade II listed building dating from the 1300s, with a barrel vaulted cellar (this maybe dating back to Norman times), a Priest's Hole and, in one of the front bedrooms, a Coffin Drop. A bricked-up doorway is thought to perhaps conceal a passageway leading to Herstmonceux Castle. There was an old-established butchery business as well, (Prickett, later Ticehurst), and a doctor resident within the village who, long ago, had his own dispensary. Now, even the *White Friars Hotel*, with its sixteenth century chimneybreast, has vanished and, sadly, Boreham Street is no longer a village but a hamlet, bearing little resemblance to its former self, save for its beautiful Sussex views, and *The Bull's Head*. (See Pages 12 and 13).

Wherever I have lived, I have always been surrounded by books and items from Hastings - many coming from the family - and I hope fervently that my memories, particularly of its past inhabitants, will never fade. Here I have barely scratched the surface. One of my father's most treasured books, from December 1955, was his signed copy, from a limited edition of only 500, of John Manwaring Baines's incomparable *Historic Hastings*. Now this, along with other material of local and often quirky interest, is in my care. I count myself privileged to have been entrusted with everything, never forgetting my father's prize for Reading awarded him by *Tower Road Infants School* on 27th March 1918, during the dark days of the First War.

Whilst writing, I have, as usual, been accompanied by the comfortable ticking of the *Pigeon Clock*, which I have known since early childhood. This was a prize won by my great-aunts at a garden fête held in St. Leonards during the First War to raise funds for our soldiers. Guessing correctly how long it would take a pigeon to travel a certain distance, their reward was a sturdy French clock of the Edwardian era, ever since referred to as the *Pigeon Clock*. Long may it continue to tick, signifying the swift passage of time and the fleeting nature of our existence. Perhaps someone, somewhere, is recording (for the benefit of future generations) impressions of the current scene within Hastings & St. Leonards. As Anne Scott remarked, so succinctly in September 2007, "History matters". Let everyone shout *Hurrah for Hastings!* with *Mr. Punch*, not wishing to be outdone, squawking, "That's the way to do it!" I hope my father's writings and photographs will stimulate discussion and raise much-needed funding for the Old Hastings Preservation Society. (See Appendix on Page 187).

MEMORIES!

Right: The Georgian Stables, Old Hastings, built c. 1746. Restored and converted into *The Stables Little Theatre*, 1958. Opened in 1959. (See Page 71). 1958 sketch by V.M. Franks.

Below left: The MTC lifeboat (shown here) was named after the wartime Mechanised (or Motor) Transport Corps, and saw sterling service at Hastings from 1950 -1964. She was the first Hastings lifeboat not to use any sail power, being motor-driven, although her overall appearance belied this fact. (See Page 70).

Below right: Launch of Hastings lifeboat with the Old Town and East Hill Lift in background, c. 1960.

Down they go—and shame on any boy who holds his nose. For grown-ups—the more enterprising ones anyway—there are the dizzy but alluring platforms of the high dive. The bathing pool at St. Leonards, built to exact proportions for international aquatic meetings, is one of the finest in Europe. At night, fireworks follow the frequent galas.

Original 1950s caption for the long-gone Bathing Pool, St. Leonards. Swimming-costumes typical of the era. Note uncomfortable, close-fitting, rubber bathing-caps. (See Page 70).

The illustration on this page, and the following three, taken from a booklet issued in the 1950s by the Publicity and Public Relations Department, County Borough of Hastings, Verulam Place. All places pictured are referred to within.

A 1950s view of Hastings Pier and Bandstand. (Original 1950s caption). (See Pages 71, 85 and 93).

Past the Pier and the Bandstand go the gaily decorated floats of the carnival procession. On the left is a corner of White Rock Pavilion, famous South Coast home of orchestral music and summer shows. In the Pier Theatre the local repertory company performs every night with weekly changes of plays.

White Rock Pavilion (now Theatre), in the 1950s.
Note trolley-bus wires and lack of traffic. (See Page 70).

The Boating Lake, Fishmarket, in the 1950s.
The young man pictured, Brian Tubbs, is now
living in New Zealand. (See Page 71 and final
paragraph of Appendix).

Children are happy as the day is long on the safe clean sands of Hastings.

(Original 1950s caption).

The beach at Hastings in the 1950s, looking eastwards towards the Pier. Note that girls are wearing dresses, not jeans or trousers. (See Page 70).

THE FESTIVAL OF BRITAIN - 1951

Front and back covers of Pauline Long's *Holiday Guide to Hastings, St. Leonards and District*, published Spring 1951 by Adams & Son of Rye, to coincide with the Festival of Britain celebrations of that year. Foreword by Malcolm Saville, well-known children's author from Hastings.

THE FESTIVAL OF BRITAIN - 1951

Two advertisements (for Hastings Pier and Mastin's Department Store) taken from *Holiday Guide to Hastings, St. Leonards and District*, published Spring 1951. (See Pages 71, 81 and 93 for Pier; Page 74 for Mastin's; and Page 73 for Plummer's).

HASTINGS PIER

(Opened 5th August, 1872) *NOW OPEN ALL DAY, EVERY DAY!*

Where you can—

★ "put another nickel in" a machine
★ try your weight
★ buy sweets, cigarettes, newspapers,
★ periodicals, fishing tackle, fruit,
★ teas, light refreshments, minerals,
★ 4-course meals, beer, wines, spirits
★ go to the theatre, dance or concert
★ enjoy a cruise in the Channel
★ a roisterous Speedboat trip
★ sit quietly and watch from a deck chair or go to a "children's hour" to see a Punch and Judy, etc.
★ hire a rod and line and go fishing
★ win a "News of the World" Rod
★ or just relax at the "Prize Game"

THE MECCA OF ENTERTAINMENT

"The Store right on the sea front"

Hundreds of holiday makers visit us year after year and are still surprised at the variety of goods displayed and our knowledge of the serious business of your relaxation.

MastinS

·7 to 12 BREEDS PLACE, HASTINGS·

SUMMARY OF INFORMATION

Accessibility. 1¾ hours by steam trains from Charing Cross and Cannon Street. Two hours by frequent electric trains from Victoria. Delightful motoring roads via Tonbridge from Central London (62½ miles) via Ashdown Forest from Western London area and via Maidstone from Eastern London area.

Area. 7,769 acres.

Aspect. Hastings : Southerly with slight inclination to East. St. Leonards : South. Town is sheltered by hills on East and North sides and is built on wooded slopes facing the sun.

Social Life. The town is exceptionally rich in clubs and societies catering for all cultural tastes. There are also clubs providing scope for social services, physical training and amusements. They range from Rotary to Judo! Full list with addresses in " Directory of Information " (apply personally or by post, Information Bureau, Hastings).

Baths. Splendidly equipped swimming baths—warmed sea water (72 degrees)—open every day throughout the year.
Luxurious medical baths including the following treatments : Hot sea water with or without blanket pack ; extract of seaweed with or without pack ; alkaline or " Anturic " with or without seaweed ; pine ; carbonated brine ; sulphur ; concentrated brine ; foam ; wax treatment ; footbath (extract of seaweed) ; aeration ; massage by qualified staff ; fully equipped electro-therapy section.

Climate. Exceptionally mild and equable for various geographical reasons. Finest in Britain for chest troubles and for recuperation. Unusual freedom from epidemics.
Prevalent wind, W.S.W. ; rainfall, averages less than 28 inches annually ; sunshine, annual average over 35 years, 1,796 hours (4.92 hours daily) ; temperature, normal mean daily range only 10.8 degrees.

Elevation. Highest point in Borough, North's Seat (600 feet).

Foundation. Sandrock, porous and speedily drained. No chalk.

Indoors

Summer shows, winter symphony concerts and recitals and stage productions in the White Rock Pavilion
Excellent repertory theatre
Seven picture theatres
Good dancing
Indoor Bowls
Roller skating
Swimming and medical baths
Internationally famous chess club
Social clubs

Municipal library
Museum and art gallery
Arts, literary and scientific clubs and societies
Bridge clubs and whist drives
Light music all the year round in the Sun Lounge
Badminton, archery, table tennis and squash racquets
N.B.—All the foregoing welcome visitors as well as residents

Outdoors

Two good 18 hole golf courses
Public tennis courts (grass and hard)
Cricket ground for county, festival and club matches
Band on Promenade in summer
Safe bathing
Magnificent bathing pool
Alfresco dancing and fireworks in summer
Finest bowls greens in Southern England

Excellent angling from Pier and boats
Pleasure cruises in Channel, boating and rowing
Foxhounds, otter hounds and harriers in close vicinity
Children's playlands and playparks with trained attendants
Putting courses, archery, football, etc.
N.B.—Residents *and* visitors welcomed by all clubs and societies

Water Supply. Drawn from wells in Ashdown Sands, also from catchment reservoirs served by an area of 3,595 acres and total storage capacity of 1,188,000,000 gallons. Comparatively soft and of excellent quality. Chalk free. Processes used selected from aeration, coagulation, rapid gravity, slow sand filtration and chlorination.

Population. 65,506 (1951 Census).

Rateable Value. £761,467 (1952-53).

Rates. (1952-53) General Rate, 19s. (compared with average of 21s. for all County Boroughs in Britain) ; Water, 3s.

Printed by F. J. Parsons Ltd., Hastings

Outside Back Cover of booklet issued 1952 - 53 by Hastings Publicity and Public Relations Department

Reproduced from *Hastings & St. Leonards Observer - Coronation Year Supplement - 1953*

(See written memories, *Jonnick Generations - Jottings - Part 2*).

Everybody knows and admires Cyril Fletcher's 'Odd Odes'. When Cyril became a member, his muse was inspired to perpetrate an Odd Ode about the Winkle Club. Cyril's Ode flouts one of the club's rules — that membership is restricted to the male sex — but nobody minded, putting it down to 'artistic license'. Here is the Ode :

Bessie from an Old Town pub
Had joined the famous Winkle Club
When 'Winkles up' was cried with zest
She raised hers higher than the rest.
She wore her winkle night and day
She wouldn't put the thing away,
Even when swimming in her vest
The winkle glistened on her chest.
One day when bathing from a float,
And here we take a doleful note,
The float upon a wave was tossed;
Up went a shout, My Winkle's lost!
A frogman drinking on the pier
Was called to leave his pint of beer,
Swam to the lady in distress
And said 'Now what's the matter Bess?'
She said: 'Oh Bill you are a toff,
I think my winkle's fallen off;
I heard a funny little clink,
I must have dropped it in the drink.'
Then Bill the frogman fixed his schnork
And on the bottom took a walk.
He searched around both far and wide,
Then surfaced on the other side
And as the float began to turn,
Saw something shine on Bessie's stern
And said 'Bess you do look daft
A-wearing of your winkle aft.'
Said Bess: 'You know it's mighty queer,
I thought a crab had nipped my rear;
When I sat down after that tinkle,
I must have sat down on my winkle.'
They pushed and turned and pulled about
But couldn't get that winkle out,
So polished it up bright and said:
'You'll have to wear it there instead.'
And now of course as you will see,
When 'Winkles up' is called with glee,
Bess doesn't shew hers as before
But blushing scuttles for the door.

THE HASTINGS WINKLE CLUB

Founded in 1900 by the fishermen of the Old Town to help the underprivileged, and still flourishing today, supporting many charities. (See Page 71).

Above: Winkle Island, Old Town. Sir Winston Churchill is shown becoming a member of the Winkle Club on 7th September 1955. Behind him is Field Marshal Montgomery standing in his open-topped desert car. Note the *Enterprise*, the last of the fishing luggers to be built at Hastings - since 1956 displayed within the Fishermen's Museum. The presentation of a solid gold winkle is being made by well-known Old Towner "Bunk" Harffey. Although not obvious from this card, over 5,000 onlookers are present, along with the Mayor of Hastings, gentlemanly Alderman F.T. Hussey, and the colourfully-robed Barons of the Cinque Ports. Many stalwarts are gathered, too, including John Burton, "Bill" and Nora Vint, and "Bill" Dyer.

Left: Extract from *Winkle Up!* - The Story of the Hastings Winkle Club by W.H. "Bill" Dyer and A.K. "Bill" Vint, published in 1972 by the Hastings Winkle Club. *Ode to a Winkle* was first publicly recited by Cyril Fletcher in Hastings (1958).

ADVERTISEMENTS TAKEN FROM 1955 REGISTER OF HOLIDAY ACCOMMODATION PUBLISHED BY HASTINGS PUBLICITY AND PUBLIC RELATIONS DEPARTMENT

In the late 1960s, when dapper Peter Franks was Manager under the Viceroy Hotels' umbrella, the Warrior Hotel, with its varying levels of labyrinthine passageways, held sedate dinner-dances on Saturdays. With unfailing regularity, proceedings wound down just before midnight with Engelbert Humperdinck's popular "hit" of the time, "The Last Waltz". Finally, the National Anthem was always played.... and then silence reigned. The Warrior advertised "fabulous value" from October to May. "For only 75/- (£3.75) you can enjoy two whole days full pension (Bed, Breakfast, Lunch and Dinner) including the Saturday night dinner-dance at which champagne prizes are given away". Afternoon tea cost 5/- (25p) and a pot of tea served at any time was priced at 1/6d (7½p) per person. (Childhood memories of the Castle Hotel appear on Page 75).

CASTLE HOTEL ●   Wellington Square (H.)

Inclusive terms:
Per week from 10 gns. to 11 gns.
These terms include bed, bath, breakfast, lunch, and evening dinner.
Licensed.

Old established, fully licensed hotel Fifty bedrooms. One minute from sea, seven minutes' walk from Hastings station. Hot and cold water and gas fires all bedrooms. Telephones each floor. Three lounges, ballroom, billiards and table tennis rooms. Lock-ups for 24 cars. Excellent food. First-class service. Cocktail lounge. Special programme at Christmas time. Telephone Hastings 344/5 and 3785. Telegraphic address: Castle Hotel, Hastings.

Resident managing directors:
Mr. and Mrs. Angus Shields.

No. 14 in register.
Facilities (see inside front cover)
ABEFGHIJKLMNOP QRT (Y-2)
Map square 1D.

WARRIOR HOTEL ● ★   Warrior Square (S.L.)

Inclusive terms:
Per week from 8 gns. to 11 gns.
These terms include bed, bath, breakfast, lunch, afternoon tea, evening dinner and coffee after dinner.
Appointed A.A. and R.A.C. Licensed.

A.A., R.A.C., fully licensed. Situated on sea front. Excellent catering and service. Modern lounges, cocktail bar, television room, games room and sun veranda. Roof garden. Fifty bedrooms with hot and cold water, interior spring mattresses, bedside telephones, gas or electric fires, central heating. Lift. Modern bathrooms. Night porter. Write for illustrated brochure and "In the centre of everything."
Telephone Hastings 3704/5.
Telegraphic address: Warrior Hotel, St. Leonards.

Proprietors:
Warrior House Hotels Ltd.

No. 13 in register.
Facilities (see inside front cover)
ABD (E†) FHIJKLMN OPQRV (Z-roof) (Y-2)
Map square 1C.

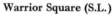

Above: Castle Hotel
Below: Royal Victoria Hotel

Above: Warrior Hotel
Below: Yelton Hotel

ROYAL VICTORIA HOTEL ● ★   Marina (S.L.)

Inclusive terms:
Per week: summer 10 gns. to 13 gns. plus 10 per cent surcharge.
Terms include bed, bath, breakfast, lunch, afternoon tea, and evening dinner. Heating, radio, telephone in all bedrooms. Dancing to Hotel orchestra, television theatre.
Appointed A.A. (four star), R.A.C.
Map square 1B.
Licensed.
No. 9 in register.
Facilities (see inside front cover)

Kings and queens have lived in this first-class hotel right on sea front. All 100 bedrooms have telephones, fitted basins, radio, central heating at no added cost. Private bathrooms. Lift all floors. Dancing to hotel orchestra. Famous Tudor bars. Billiards. Television theatre. Comfortable lounges. Private television in many bedrooms. Half rates from 1st October to end of May—6½ gns. plus 10 per cent.
Telephone Hastings 3300.
Telegraphic address: Royal Vic, St. Leonards.

Proprietor: J. Bartholomew.
General manager: A. Lawrence.

ABCD (E†) FGHIJKLNOPQRT (T†) V (Y—2, 3, 4).

YELTON HOTEL ●   White Rock (H.)

Inclusive terms:
Per week from 8½ gns. to 11½ gns.
These terms include bed, bath, breakfast, lunch, afternoon tea, evening dinner, and coffee after dinner.
Licensed.
A.A. R.A.C.

Next to White Rock Pavilion, opposite pier, bandstand and sea. Bowling greens, tennis courts, indoor swimming baths within three minutes' walk. All forty-six bedrooms have running hot and cold water, Vi-spring mattresses, gas or electric fires; some have balconies facing seawards. Lounge faces front with sheltered balcony. Excellent cuisine. Resident proprietors. Cocktail lounge. Lift. Night porter. Telephone Hastings 2240.

Resident proprietors:
Mrs. M. A. Bouquet, Mr. and Mrs. N. A. Eccles.

No. 15 in register.
Facilities (see inside front cover)
ABD (E†) FGHIJKLN PQRT
Map square 1D.

FAREWELL TO STEAM

EVENING ARGUS, 7/6/58   9

LAST OF THE LINE

The last London - bound steam passenger train will pull out of Hastings Station tomorrow.

As from Monday, full-scale diesel electric services will operate on the Hastings-London run.

Picture shows one of the last steam trains, with a Schools class engine, leaving Hastings for Charing Cross.

(See Pages 41, 91 and 182).

Right: Reproduced from Southern Region Leaflet BR35034/1 announcing Revised Train Services between London and Hastings, via Tunbridge Wells, effective 17th June 1957.

Better Services between London and Hastings

On Monday, 17th June 1957, the first stage of the Southern Region's diesel electrification scheme for the London/Hastings line via Tunbridge Wells will come into being, although the full effect of the radical changes planned will not be apparent until the final completion in June 1958.

Three existing steam trains up in the morning and down again in the evening on the "business-hour" services will be replaced by four diesel-electric trains providing 2,000 seats against the present 1,550 in each direction during these particular periods— an increase of 30% in accommodation.

One of these new trains will do the journey in 90 minutes in each direction. Certain other off-peak services will be operated by the new trains, giving accelerated journey times.

To provide for the additional trains schedules have had to be revised and this means that certain down main line trains in the evening business period will no longer call at London Bridge Station. It is realised that this, unfortunately, will not be so convenient to some of our passengers, but, whilst we regret this, the new services will benefit the majority.

By June 1958, all steam trains on the London/Hastings line will have been replaced by diesel-electric trains of modern design, constructed to make the best possible use of the restricted width of carriage imposed by the narrow tunnels on this route.

Although trains on the Bexhill West line will remain steam operated for the present, it is hoped to replace them with diesel units next year when the remainder of the steam trains on the Hastings line will also be replaced.

On the reverse of this folder is a complete timetable starting on Monday, 17th June, 1957, including the new diesel-electric "business-hour" services.

Any further information can be obtained from:—

Chief Commercial Manager, or
Waterloo Station,
London, S.E.1
(Telephone: WATerloo 5151)

District Traffic Supt.,
Orpington,
Kent
(Telephone: Orpington 25724)

COUNTY BOROUGH OF HASTINGS SWIMMING CERTIFICATE

Issued to Cynthia Scrivens 2nd August 1959. Signed by J. Ryper (Instructor) and F. D. Boone (Manager), Hastings Baths.
(See Page 69).

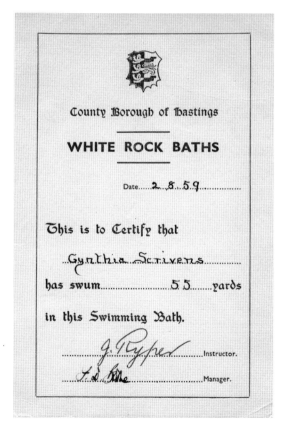

County Borough of Hastings

WHITE ROCK BATHS

Date... 2 . 8 . 5 9 ...

This is to Certify that

Cynthia Scrivens

has swum..............55..........yards

in this Swimming Bath.

..........J. Ryper........Instructor.

..........F. D. Boone........Manager.

1950s - THE SOUND OF STEAM

Record Sleeve Illustration by R. C. Riley showing *Christ's Hospital* leaving Cannon Street with a train for Hastings.

Directed by Peter Handford, this extended play vinyl record (EAF 76), issued by the Argo Record Company in 1963, marked the passing of steam travel. Identified Schools' class 4-4-0s of the Southern Railway were recorded at work and facing varying conditions on the Hastings line during the 1950s. We also hear evocative loudspeaker system passenger information, engine whistling and air-operated hooter noises, as well as boys on a platform who mimic cattle penned in a nearby truck. Smoke and gleaming engines come to mind! (See Pages 41, 90 and 182).

Below left: Photograph and detail taken from "100 Years of Progress", a history of the **Hastings Permanent Building Society,** published in 1949. Founded in 1849, the exact name of the Society varied over the years but, in 1884, it became known as The Rape of Hastings Mutual Permanent Benefit Building Society. In 1908 the title of Hastings Permanent Building Society was adopted. The photograph shows early office premises in Oak Passage, High Street: built in 1865, the date appears above the doorway. The premises were very small and the accommodation provided cramped desk room for three people. If a visitor arrived, the junior clerk had to leave the office due to lack of space! (See Page 44).

Below centre and right: Two advertisements reproduced from "Souvenir Catalogue for the Hastings Embroidery", published by Hastings Publicity & Public Relations Department in connection with the 1966 celebrations surrounding the 900th Anniversary of the Battle of Hastings. The **Hastings & East Sussex Building Society** (founded 1851) and the Model Village, White Rock Gardens, are referred to on Pages 76 and 72 respectively.

Hastings Permanent B.S. Office in Oak Passage

Hastings and East Sussex

BUILDING SOCIETY

Founded 1851

ASSETS	RESERVES
£17,000,000	£800,000

ASSURED SECURITY FOR INVESTORS

HOME LOANS

WELLINGTON PLACE, HASTINGS   Tel. 28261
(3 lines)

ST. LEONARDS-ON-SEA: 22 NORMAN ROAD
BEXHILL-ON-SEA: 44 ST. LEONARDS ROAD
BATTLE: 34 HIGH STREET
ASHFORD (Kent): 65 HIGH STREET
FOLKESTONE: 17 GUILDHALL STREET
MAIDSTONE: 20/22 KING STREET

Shares and Deposits in the Society are Trustee Investments

MEMBER OF THE BUILDING SOCIETIES ASSOCIATION

The Hastings Embroidery traces the History of Britain in Pictorial Form—now visit the . . .

Model Village

WHITE ROCK GARDENS, opposite the Pier

. . . TO SEE THE BEAUTY OF ALL BRITAIN IN ONE HALF ACRE OF LANDSCAPE GARDENS AND MINUTELY DETAILED ARCHITECTURAL MODELS. MINIATURE PLANTS AND SHRUBS ARE ALSO A FEATURE.

Open Every Day of the Year

PARTIES WELCOME

The Hastings Embroidery - Panel 1
The Battle of Hastings with the Hastings Coat of Arms

(See Pages 71, 81 and 85 for other Pier detail).

Working on the Hastings Embroidery at the Royal School of Needlework.
Photograph by British Travel Association

THE TRIODOME, HASTINGS PIER

Detail and Pictures from "Souvenir Catalogue for the Hastings Embroidery", published by Hastings Publicity & Public Relations Department.

In the run-up to the 900th Anniversary of the Battle of Hastings, the Triodome was specifically commissioned to house the Hastings Embroidery and Model of the 1066 Battlefield. At the time of construction, it was the largest building of its type in the United Kingdom. Sited at the entrance to Hastings Pier, it was a specially designed, light-weight, portable building, and was firmly bolted to the pier decking.

The Royal School of Needlework produced a remarkable historical embroidery (*not* a tapestry) showing some of the most important events in the history of the country during the previous 900 years, this comprising 27 panels consisting of 81 pictures. It was a great success and proved hugely popular, being seen by a quarter of a million people in 1966.

Bill's crusty loaves may soon disappear

ANOTHER LOAD FOR THE OVEN

MR BECK feeds another batch of rolls into his 112-year-old oven which has to be changed by order soon

THE ALBERT MEMORIAL, HASTINGS - c. 1960

Trolley-buses were replaced in 1959 by the powerful Atlantean (Maidstone & District) buses, one of which is seen behind the Memorial (sadly demolished in 1973) travelling eastwards away from us. Trolley-bus wires still visible. Little traffic about.

Photograph of Mr. Beresford "Bill" Beck, the well-known baker of East Ascent, St. Leonards, alongside his solid brick, coal-fired oven installed in 1860. (See Page 72).

SPONGE & LUNCHEON CAKES DAILY

W. A. BECK & SON.

Fancy Bread & Biscuit Bakers,

Nº 6, EAST ASCENT,

Sᵀ LEONARDS.

A SPECIALITY. HOME MADE BREAD.

TELEPHONE Nº 857.

W. A. BECK & SON, BAKERS

Paper-Bag - very early 20th century

Features Victorian engraving of lively, crowded scene on, and around, Hastings Pier. Much "promenading, meeting and greeting" activity on Pier by both sexes of all ages, as was usual then. Some, however, are seated, enjoying the sea-breezes. Horse-drawn transport evident, as expected, and exuberant dog in foreground! (See facing page, and Page 72 for full detail on Beck family business, plus link with Princess Victoria).

OLD HASTINGS

Alone I climb the hill and see the town
Sombre and leaden; here and there a spire
Or a small turret juts acuter, higher -
A road that puckers through it like a frown;
A single cart that rattles up and down;
A wisp of chimney-smoke, some struggling fire;
And faint the shouting of an earlier Crier -
All colours moulded in a misty brown.

I love it, this old town, wedged with such grace
Between its hills. On one the Castle seems
To hold suggestions of eternity;
This corner of the world - a simple face
Lovely in smiling age - a haunt of dreams -
A bit of England as she used to be!

Rupert Croft-Cooke

Leonard Scrivens
1911 - 1992

Photograph taken in June, 1914, at the
U.S.A. Studios, 1, 3 and 5 Palace Avenue,
White Rock, Hastings.

— ❦ Foreword to Photographic Plates ❦ —

The photographs which form the basis for the following notes were, in the main, collected by locally-born Mr. Crowhurst. Mr. Crowhurst offered his Album, and other material, to Mr. Stephen Samuelson, bookseller of Claremont, from whom, in 1978, I acquired the Album.

Hastings & St. Leonards is predominantly a Victorian town, and its growth during the 19th century was truly phenomenal. Nothing shows this more clearly than the population figures:

1801	3,175	(date of the first official Census)
1811	4,025	
1831	10,231	
1861	23,443	
1891	59,784	
1901	65,528	

In fact, as a map by John Flower in the book *Literary Landscapes of the British Isles* shows, only two non-industrial towns in the country grew at such a rate - Brighton and Hastings - such growth otherwise being restricted to South Wales, the Midlands and North. Locally, if one excludes the Old Town, Joseph Kay's work on the seafront and at Belmont, and Burton's St. Leonards, the Queen's reign saw all major expansion. Sadly, much of the earlier (pre -1837) work has been replaced, at Pelham Place in the 1890s by the Palace of Varieties (ironically, a period piece in its own right); at Marina in the 1930s by Marine Court; and at Breeds Place in the 1960s and 1970s by insensitive office blocks. Worst of all was the disembowelment of the Old Town by the Corporation to create a new road (The Bourne) in post-War years - described in *Buildings of England, Sussex* (Professor Nikolaus Pevsner & Ian Nairn) as "The Rape of Hastings indeed". On a purely practical note, though, how would present-day traffic cope if restricted to the narrow High Street and All Saints Street, for the post-War Bourne forms part of the A 259, the main coast road.

Finally, few realise today but, as I have said before, at the turn of the 20th century, Hastings, with St. Leonards, was the second largest seaside resort in the United Kingdom, second only to Brighton. Although by then in some decline, St. Leonards, which not many years before had been the most fashionable small seaside town in the country, was still much favoured. These pictures, the earliest of which date from the 1850s, to my mind emphasise the virtues of Victorian planning and building, which despite its faults was, at its best, very much to be preferred to most of what has been built since, particularly in the years since the last War.

LEONARD SCRIVENS (written 1978/79)

My father noted subsequently:

"In the Annual Report of the Hastings and St. Leonards Museum Association submitted on 7th December 1981, under *Acquisitions* it was stated 'The Crowhurst Collection of Oils, Watercolours, Pen and Ink Drawings, Sketches, Engravings, Pamphlets, Notices, etc., was purchased by the Went Tree Trust and Victoria and Albert Purchase Grant Fund'."

Copies of a number of the photographic plates were taken by Hastings Library, and by other parties, in 1978. It is believed that some have been reproduced in publications elsewhere.

C. W.

Textual Information on Photographic Plates

Plate 1   Page 99
ALL SAINTS CHURCH AND THE OLD TOWN
This very early print shows All Saints prior to the "restoration" of 1870, and also gives a clear view of the back of the Rectory. The distant West Hill is undeveloped (save for what could be Plynlimmon) and, with three mills shown, it dates from the early 1850s.

Plate 2   Page 100
ALL SAINTS CHURCH
Probably similar in date to Plate 1 showing All Saints Church and the Old Town, or even earlier. Showing in detail the condition of the tower, roof and porch prior to the "restoration" of 1870.

Plate 3   Page 101
ST. CLEMENT'S CHURCH
Probably taken in the early 1890s, with the flank wall of The Swan to the left. The Swan Inn, High Street, dated back to 1523, although there are 14th century site references. Greatly favoured in the 18th and 19th centuries, The Swan was a celebrated coaching inn and hosted all of the town's important functions, William Scrivens becoming landlord in 1779. Rebuilt in 1879, it became the Swan Public House, and was destroyed during the air-raid of 23rd May 1943. The site is now laid out as a garden of remembrance.

Note the large wall advertisement on the right-hand house - not unusual up to the First World War. Is it a battleship? And what did it advertise?

Plate 4   Page 102
TACKLEWAY
Nothing whatever to do with tackle (fishing or otherwise). Shown as "le tegill wey" in a deed of 1499, and probably meaning "the tiled way" or "the way to the tile kilns" according to J.M. Baines. At one time a favoured residential area known as East Hill Walk, it had by 1857 declined in favour.

In that year, George Macdonald, the writer, took a house he renamed "Huntly Cottage" and, in a letter, wrote "pretty, but not in a fashionable part of the town". (He was born in Huntly).

Plates 5 and 6   Page 103
FROM THE ROEBUCK YARD
Originally, and at least from 1742, The Starr, but from 1840 The Roebuck. The "putting up" place for many of the local carriers in Victorian days, and a service which lasted until 1939. Demolished with the making of the Bourne through-road and the clearances in the Old Town then effected.

Now Roebuck Street links High Street with the Bourne and, on the approximate site of the inn, is Roebuck House, a group medical practice building.

Through the arch can be seen No. 90 High Street, the home of clockmaker William Gill, and the site of the first Bank in Hastings. *(See text detail on Pages 174 and 175 for Plate 67).*

(5) As photographed by Arthur Moulton. Here the fascia board for No. 90 High Street reads "W. WH...". Pike's Directory for 1876 lists "W. White, tobacconist, etc.", at this address and, for 1894, "W. White, newsagent and photographer."

(6) As depicted in postcard form by Charles Graves, 1834/35 - 1918, noted artist from St. Leonards.

Plate 7   Page 104
THE STADE (LOOKING EAST)
The East Hill Lift of 1902 is not shown, neither is there any sign of the Harbour works of 1896.

What is particularly noticeable is the small area of beach - presumably the harbour arm, over the years, acted as a very large groyne and the "eastward drift", in the 20th century, created the huge accumulation of beach extending from Denmark Place eastwards.

Plate 1 ALL SAINTS CHURCH AND THE OLD TOWN Text on Page 98

ALL SAINTS CHURCH

Plate 2

Plate 3 ST. CLEMENT'S CHURCH **Text on Page 98**

Plate 4   **TACKLEWAY**   **Text on Page 98**

Plates 5 and 6 FROM THE ROEBUCK YARD **Text on Page 98**

Plate 7 THE STADE (LOOKING EAST) Text on Page 98

Plate 8   **THE STADE (NEAR TO THE FISHMARKET) LOOKING WEST**   Text on Page 106

Plate 8   **Page 105**

THE STADE (NEAR TO THE FISHMARKET) LOOKING WEST

The Victorian Retail Fishmarket can be seen to the left of The Queen's Head. This corrugated iron octangular building, The Rotunda of 1870, stood in the centre of the road at the foot of the High Street and was demolished in the 1920s, when trolley-buses came to the town and increasing traffic made usage difficult.

The Queen's Head in East Beach Street was first licensed in 1830 and was closed in 1913 (according to J.M. Baines). It was said to be popular with Victorian visitors, and traders whose goods brought in by sea were unloaded nearby.

The gantry was to carry signal lights at night, and the fishing industry was then one of considerable size. One can see how busy the scene would have been by the large number of Hastings "flats" (two-wheeled handcarts), the three to four ice-crushing machines in view, and the barrels waiting to be filled. The sign "Adams Refreshment Rooms" reminds us that this family is still important locally.

Plates 9, 10, 11 and 12   **Pages 108 - 111**

THE EASTERN BEACHES, THE STADE AND THE HARBOUR

These four very detailed photographs were all taken in the later 1890s and show construction of the ill-fated Harbour in hand.

The history of harbours here since the earliest days is a sad tale. The four pictures all relate to a scheme propounded in 1889, the Act for which received the Royal Assent in 1890, the plans having been drawn up by a Mr. Richard Hassard. Briefly, the overwhelming difficulty (as ever) was to raise the money required but, eventually, sanction was given by the Board of Trade and the tender submitted by Messrs. Punchard, McTaggart, Lowther & Company was accepted, work commencing in 1896. However, as further hoped-for essential funding was not forthcoming, work ceased in 1897 and was never completed. There was talk of construction being suspended when a large and very deep mudhole barred further progress but, in truth, it was just a case of under-capitalisation.

Until the last war, a Harbour office and works were maintained at Mercers Bank, Fishmarket, but this establishment disappeared during the war years, and Mercers Bank itself (an historic name) also vanished as a result of post-war highway construction.

In connection with the doomed scheme, plans were made for the building of the Hastings Harbour District Railway Company. This was to proceed from the Harbour Station along the seashore to Ecclesbourne Glen. There it would run through a tunnel to a station at Harold Road, thence by another tunnel to a station at Ore. There would be further stations at Kites Nest (for St. Helens) and Grove Road (for Silverhill). The S. E. R. line would be joined at Harley Shute with a connection to West St. Leonards Station (S. E.). The cost of this line would have been immense and, even if constructed, would most probably have suffered annual damage from both sea and land. It was opposed from the start by, amongst others, the Dannreuthers (newly established at "Windycroft", High Wickham) and, fortunately for us all, the scheme never got off the ground.

Plate 9 shows a derrick or pile-driver on the Stade, presumably at the very beginning of the project (timber is being stacked to the right). Although there is a reasonable amount of beach, the photograph was, I think, taken at half tide and the lifeboat house of 1882 was, therefore, well placed.

Plate 10 shows construction of the western harbour pier well under way, and seems to have been taken at about high water. Note the twin-funnelled paddle-steamer making for Hastings Pleasure Pier, a summer service which, although twice interrupted by War, lasted until the late 1950s. See also washing drying flat on the shingle (the custom then) as well as being line-dried on the beach.

Plate 11, looking east, shows the western arm again, and what I think is a photographic "mock-up" of the proposed eastern pier. This never got very far (although extended as a groyne in the 1950s) but, on the landward end, a red granite stone dated the harbour effort and quoted the name of Alderman Bradnam - maybe Chairman of the Commissioners. This print clearly shows the roof of the Retail Fishmarket (demolished in the 1920s), the Dust Destructor Chimney (demolished in the 1930s), and Scrivens Buildings (demolished in 1978). The tower of the lifeboat house stands out, as does the advertisement for George Mence Smith, the oil and colour man, who also had a grocery business here. In addition, he had shops in Bohemia and London Road, St. Leonards, and was an early "multiple", hailing from S.E. London. Nearby, in George Street, lived Mr. T. Boucher who must be mentioned - he surely deserved a place in Dickens, being described in Pike's 1894 Directory as "Greengrocer, fireman, comedian, ETC." In the foreground, the upper part of the "100 Steps" leading to the West Hill.

Plate 12 shows Civil Engineering of the 1890s at close quarters, and very primitive it looks - a steam crane is unloading from a coaster and the contractor's light railway engine hauls a ballast train. Incidentally, according to J.M. Baines, writing in respect of the plan devised by Mr. Carey, the engineer, "The piers were to be constructed of concrete on the monolithic principle and, when completed, each would really be a smooth and solid block of rock jutting out into the Channel, offering no crevice to the action of the waves and holding no mortar-bound stones for the currents to drag from their positions".

Plate 13	Page 112

THE STADE (NEAR TO THE FISHMARKET) LOOKING EAST

The lifeboat was housed at Rock-a-Nore Road, moving in 1882 to East Parade, as here shown. The first Hastings lifeboat was built in the mid-1830s by Thwaites & Winter, the highly-skilled George Tutt (eventually with his own business) being one of their employees. The Royal National Lifeboat Institution took over in 1858. With the ever-growing accumulation of beach at East Parade, the Lifeboat House again moved to the seaward side of East Beach Street.

The Pelican Inn shown on the left of the picture was in Commercial Road. This never very long road was, with closure and demolition, eventually reduced to just two buildings which were renumbered and taken into High Street.

Plate 14	Page 113

NORTH-EAST FROM THE WEST HILL

Innumerable photographs have been taken from the East Hill, looking south-west over the Old Town to the sea.

This photograph, unusually, is taken from the West Hill, probably above Croft Road, looking inland to the north-east, and dates, I should think, from the late 1890s.

On the right, All Saints Church. Nearer, St. Mary Star of the Sea, poet Coventry Patmore's memorial to his second wife. Designed by Basil Champneys and completed in 1883 (according to Derek Patmore, "Portrait of my Family", 1935) it was much praised by Pevsner.

Beyond, the thickly gorsed East Hill, with, near the skyline, High Wickham, originally Prospect Place, and built largely by Humphrey Wickham, the butcher, in the 1820s.

This row of houses, with its significant position, had great appeal for writers and artists in Victorian and Edwardian times. George Mogridge ("Old Humphrey"), Mrs. Betham Edwards, William Hale White ("Mark Rutherford"), Thomas Parkin, Harry Furniss and Professor Dannreuther, were all residents.

To the left, Belmont, with Villas by Joseph Kay, the architect of Pelham Crescent. They date from about 1830. Further to the left, the growing district of Clive Vale, with the spire of Clive Vale Congregational Church dating from the 1880s. Beyond, green fields, but these remained longer than sometimes - often until the 1950s.

Plate 15	Page 114

MARINE PARADE AND PIER ROCKS

This very early photograph, taken at low water from the beach at Marine Parade and looking west, shows (left to right) a corner pavilion on the Queen's Hotel (1858/62, according to Pevsner), Beach Terrace (demolished between the wars for Parade improvements), Pelham Crescent and Pelham Place, Gunner Ross's Cottage (Ross was the last to hold the post of Town Gunner), the opening to George Street and the Albion Hotel.

The rocks and timbers in the foreground are remains of the pier built in 1595 by experts from Lyme Regis and destroyed by the sea almost immediately. Rebuilt in 1597, it was "overthrown by the sea in less than an hour", and although plans were made by a Dutchman to build afresh in 1635, nothing developed. The rocks were probably last seen when the Parade and road hereabouts were remade in the 1930s.

Plate 9

THE EASTERN BEACHES, THE STADE AND THE HARBOUR

Text on Page 106

Plate 10 THE EASTERN BEACHES, THE STADE AND THE HARBOUR **Text on Page 106**

Plate 11   THE EASTERN BEACHES, THE STADE AND THE HARBOUR   Text on Page 106

Plate 12 **THE EASTERN BEACHES, THE STADE AND THE HARBOUR** Text on Page 107

Plate 13 THE STADE (NEAR TO THE FISHMARKET) LOOKING EAST Text on Page 107

Plate 14   **NORTH-EAST FROM THE WEST HILL**   Text on Page 107

Plate 15   MARINE PARADE AND PIER ROCKS   **Text on Page 107**

Plate 16 THE CASTLE HILL **Text on Page 116**

Plate 16   **Page 115**

THE CASTLE HILL

Taken at low water and probably a little later in date than that of the Pier Rocks, showing Caroline Place (damaged and finally demolished after the last war), Breeds Place (demolished and redeveloped in the 1960s), Pelham Crescent and Beach Terrace.

Between Beach Terrace and George Street can be seen a flagpole, probably used by the coastguards for storm-warning signals.

Plate 17   **Page 118**

THE SANDS AND CASTLE HILL

This very busy scene at low water shows the seafront from Harold Place to Breeds Place, all buildings but The Carlisle having long since been demolished. The seafront from west to east was here known as Denmark Place, Carlisle Villas, Caroline Parade and finally Caroline Place. All save the Public House have now gone and only the name Denmark Place remains.

The post-war rebuilding of Castle Street (after allowing for road widening on the sea-front) meant the extinction of Caroline Place, with what was left being known throughout as Denmark Place.

Plate 18   **Page 119**

THE CASTLE

Taken in 1895 and looking to the west, this view has changed but little at the time of writing (1978/79). The Queen's has lost its corner pavilions, Hastings Pier has been rebuilt between the wars (following the fire of 1917), and St. Leonards Pier, damaged during the Second World War, was finally demolished in 1951.

Plate 19   **Page 120**

THE CASTLE HILL

This photograph by Francis Frith & Co. must be of the 1890s, (Palace Pier, St. Leonards, shown). Note the lack of development in Cambridge Road, once past Holmesdale Gardens.

Plate 20   **Page 121**

TO THE NORTH-WEST FROM THE CASTLE HILL

This print dates from about 1880 and unfortunately most detail is poor. Difficulty also arises due to subsequent development of the West Hill

and switching of street names - variations of "Castle", "Castle Hill", plus "Avenue", "Terrace", "Hill", "Road", etc.

In the foreground, the upper part of Castle Road, which became Castle Hill Road, with an entrance to Castledown House. This was the home of the Rev. William Wallinger, first "Perpetual Curate" of St. Mary-in-the-Castle (1828/34). It continued in single occupation until the 1900s, but later was converted into flats - the change probably being hastened by the cutting of the present Castledown Avenue at the turn of the 20th century, and the building of maisonettes on the north-western side. Subsequently, the house remained empty and derelict for some years.

Beyond the house, but unseen, is Wallinger's Walk, with, on the corner, the old St. Mary-in-the-Castle burial ground. This Walk, from Castle Hill Road to the Hill, was shortened when Castledown Avenue was cut through to Wellington Road in the early part of the 20th century.

In the middle distance, the Gas Works and Headquarters of the old Hastings & St. Leonards Gas Company. Gas was manufactured on this site prior to 1832 when the company was formed. It paid its predecessors in title £12,000 for an undertaking whose sales in that year amounted to $2\frac{1}{2}$ million cubic feet. Manufacture here continued until 1907, when all working was transferred to Glyne Gap.

To the right, the tower of St. Andrew's Church, built and brought into use in 1870, and the gift of Miss Sayer, a connection of the Milward family. After just about 100 years the church was demolished and replaced by a filling station. Whatever would Miss Sayer, or her kinswoman, Countess Waldegrave, of the Mansion, have said, particularly the latter who spent her life endowing churches - she must have turned in her grave.

A point of interest is that the building contained wall paintings by Robert Tressell, author of "The Ragged Trousered Philanthropists" who, at one time, lived in Milward Road nearby.

Just beyond can be seen the embankment of the Ashford - Hastings (S.E.) Railway line with what appears to be an early goods train. The line, opened in 1851, was the first rail link with Hastings proper. This is a testing bank all the way from the Goods Yard to Coghurst, much at 1 in 60, and even the powerful diesel engines (used for summertime weekend specials) could slip badly on a greasy day.

On the other side of the railway and to the left, the beginnings of Park

Road (now Lower Park Road), and between this and the sinuous newly-built terrace of St. Helen's Road, what would then be St. Andrew's Gardens, extended and formally opened as Alexandra Park in 1882 by the Prince and Princess of Wales, but remembered even earlier by grandfather as a farm with a hop-garden.

Further to the right, Baldslow Road, Elphinstone Road climbing to the Langham, Quarry Road and the Blacklands area - beyond that, still mainly fields, but very often not for long.

Population   1851 - 16,966
              1901 - 65,528

Plate 21   Page 122
CHRIST CHURCH, BLACKLANDS

This shows the church before the building of the tower.

The Blacklands Estate was developed by Charles Hay Frewen of Coghurst in the 1870s. A church was deemed essential and Frewen gave the site, started the church and had partly built a parsonage when he died in 1878. As he had made no arrangements for an endowment, the Bishop would not consecrate the building which rapidly deteriorated. The original developer's trustees wished for a Church of England parish church and, following a threat of passing the unfinished building to the Nonconformists, and agreeing on a modest endowment, the Bishop relented, and the church was consecrated in 1881.

The Estate was a success, the church became popular with many prosperous members and, in 1891, the tower, thought by some to be disproportionately large, was added.

Plate 22   Page 123
BEHIND HIGH WICKHAM

Golf was first played in Hastings in 1893, and Pike's Directory for 1894 shows the Hastings & St. Leonards Golf Club at No. 3 High Wickham.

The Club was started with £150 and permission was given by the Corporation to use the East Hill. The site (part of which is shown here) ran from High Wickham to the top of the Hill and down the slope to Barley Lane in the north-west.

Later, with the help of the Rev. Sayer-Milward, the original seven holes were extended to nine. The first President was Sayer-Milward, Dr. Frith was Captain and Joint Secretary with Dr. Christopherson, and these, with Harry Furniss, formed the Committee.

Over the years, the Club extended and moved the course several times. It also used three clubhouses, the last being Fishponds Farmhouse but, always short of money, it eventually closed down.

In the centre of the picture we see Harold Road climbing the hill to Ore and, from right to left, Dudley Road. This joins Ashburnham Road which can be seen curving uphill to its upper junction with Old London Road.

Further north are the Githa Road Schools and Clive Vale Congregational Church in Edwin Road.

Many open fields await the developer.

Plate 23   Page 124
PELHAM PLACE

This very fine print shows, from left to right, No. 9, the second premises of the Hastings Old Bank (and home of George Scrivens of the Old Bank), later the Sandringham Hotel.

At the far right, the once well-known Marine (or Royal Marine) Hotel. This house, when under the management of C.P. Hutchins, became famous, and the Empress Eugenie made it her residence when exiled from France in 1870. Dr. Granville ("Spas of England", 1841) put up here; he gave a good report and mentions that the charge was 7/6d (37$^{1}/_{2}$p) per day! In the late 1890s the premises were demolished to make way for the Palace of Varieties, later the Cinema de Luxe, and eventually the Amusement Centre.

Beyond this may be seen the Coastguards' quarters and the opening to George Street. The Russian Gun (from the Crimea) remained until the Second World War when it was taken for scrap. Behind this stands a bathchair, these being until the 1930s a common sight - providing a living for quite a few. Pike's Directory shows five "Bath Chair Proprietors" in 1894, three in 1915, and none in 1932. They seem as improbable today as the sedan chair!

227628 Hastings, Sands & Castle Hill

Plate 17   THE SANDS AND CASTLE HILL   **Text on Page 116**

Plate 18

THE CASTLE

Text on Page 116

Plate 19　　　　　　　　　　　　**THE CASTLE HILL**　　　　　　　　　　　　**Text on Page 116**

Plate 20 TO THE NORTH-WEST FROM THE CASTLE HILL **Text on Page 116**

Plate 21 CHRIST CHURCH, BLACKLANDS Text on Page 117

Plate 22　　　　　　　　　　　**BEHIND HIGH WICKHAM**　　　　　　　　　　　**Text on Page 117**

1600. *Hastings. Pelham Place.*

Plate 23

PELHAM PLACE

Text on Page 117

Plate 24   **Page 126**

PELHAM CRESCENT AND BEACH TERRACE

To the left, Breeds Place, built by Lansdell in the 1820s and replaced by hideous office blocks. We see Pelham Crescent and St. Mary-in-the-Castle, with, in the foreground, the premises of Messrs. Ellis, Wilson & Vidler.

To the right, Beach Terrace - demolished for Parade and road improvements in the 1930s. Always at the mercy of the weather, Pike's Directory for 1876 lists six occupants and adds "other houses rendered untenable by the floods", this no doubt referring to the great storm in November 1875 which caused extensive seafront damage (see Cousins, "Hastings of Bygone Days - And the Present", Page 237). The terrace includes a Primitive Methodist Hall. Chapelgoers were tough in those days! Date -1876.

Plate 25   **Page 127**

PELHAM CRESCENT AND BREEDS PLACE

Well detailed for architectural ironwork and probably of the same date as Plate 24, showing Pelham Crescent and Beach Terrace. Already 15 Pelham Crescent is a shop - possibly Pocock Brothers for boots.

Plate 26   **Page 128**

CAROLINE PLACE AWASH AND BEACH TERRACE UNDER WATER

Caroline Place on left - Beach Terrace in distance. Photograph possibly taken during the storm of November 1875.

Plate 27   **Page 129**

CAROLINE PLACE
(Caroline Parade more to the West)

The whole of this seafront group of eating houses, lodging houses and teashops has gone, following wartime bombing and later demolition, the sole surviving building being The Carlisle. Caroline Place faced the sea in front of Castle Street and ended at approximately the position of the present roundabout, (1978/79).

The bathchair shown appears to be a very heavy, early model, with cart-like wheels and when in use would give hard work to the chairman, particularly on hills. Beyond may be seen what appears to be a camera tripod and, nearer, some form of wheeled sales stall with a bucket beneath - coffee or shellfish?

Plate 28   **Page 130**

CARLISLE PARADE

A peaceful scene in the 1890s which lasted until 1930, never to return; also a bathchair rank. The buildings have changed very little, the only modern intrusion being Albany Court (1961/63), built following wartime bombing - even Pevsner ("Buildings of England - Sussex") considered this replacement to be "very tactfully done"!

The Lion and Unicorn still to be seen opposite Robertson Terrace were, according to Cousins (Page 220 of "Hastings of Bygone Days - And the Present"), "removed from Buckingham Palace on account of certain objections, other animals being substituted and the originals brought to Hastings".

Plate 29   **Page 131**

THE CENTRAL PARADES

(A) Carlisle Parade showing many of the necessary late Victorian needs for a seaside holiday - sailing boats, bathchairs (with summer hoods), bathing-machines, Punch and Judy (perhaps "Professor" Blazier), and a beach photographer's tripod.

(B) White Rock on a sunny day, all, even the youngest, well wrapped-up, and much use of umbrellas to keep off the sun! Also, a good showing of top hats and walking sticks!

(C) West of Hastings Pier and an earlier photograph. At this time there were railings on the road side of the Parade, but not on the sea side. Seating mid-Victorian, Pier as originally built (without excrescences).

(D) White Rock Corner and again Hastings Pier as built - hawker selling balloons?

Plate 24 **PELHAM CRESCENT AND BEACH TERRACE** **Text on Page 125**

Plate 25　　　　　　　PELHAM CRESCENT AND BREEDS PLACE　　　　　　　**Text on Page 125**

Plate 26   CAROLINE PLACE AWASH AND BEACH TERRACE UNDER WATER   **Text on Page 125**

Plate 27   **CAROLINE PLACE** (Caroline Parade more to the West)   **Text on Page 125**

Plate 28 **CARLISLE PARADE** **Text on Page 125**

(A) Carlisle Parade

(B) White Rock

(C) West of Hastings Pier

(D) White Rock Corner

Plate 29

THE CENTRAL PARADES

Text on Page 125

(A)

(B)

(C)

(D)

Plate 31 **AROUND THE MEMORIAL** **Text on Page 134**

Plate 30   **Page 132**

DURING THE 1860s

A very clear, very pleasing and very early photograph taken when the Queen's Hotel and Carlisle Parade were newly built. The Lion and Unicorn which flanked the private gardens of Robertson Terrace had only recently been brought from London, and the photograph appears to have been taken early in the morning.

The brigantine beached opposite Caroline Place is a reminder that until about 1880 coal, timber and general goods were brought to the town by sea.

Plate 31   **Page 133**

AROUND THE MEMORIAL

(A) From left to right, first a corner of the Music Hall, later the Public Hall, for some years a cinema (latterly the Orion) and eventually closed. Next, the Havelock Public House, then obviously more extensive and using the corner premises for hotel purposes. Opposite, the Hastings branch of the London & County Bank, removed here from George Street, and the first joint stock bank in the town. A new building was put up on the same site in the 1930s by the Westminster Bank as successors to the London County Westminster & Parr's Bank Ltd., becoming, in time, a branch of the National Westminster Bank. Adjoining, Bank Buildings of 1862 and, beneath the voluminous shop blind, Geo. Reeves, shoe and leather warehouse. This building was also replaced before the Second World War by Burton, the tailor.

The Memorial itself, often under threat in post-war years by a short-sighted and indeterminate local authority, was finally entered by vandals, set afire, and later declared dangerous and demolished in 1973 - a great loss and an almost unbelievable story.

(B) From left to right, the York, formerly Hayters, carrying the Arms of the City of London - in the 1890s owned by the London Distillery Company. Then York Buildings, Wellington Place, Pelham Street and Denmark Place. The latter, well-known for Lewcocks Eating House, suffered extensive war damage. On the right is the corner of Harold Place and Robertson Street, the site, for so many years, of Amoore, the grocer.

(C) A much older photograph, (early 1870s), and, from left to right, first Reeves, shoe and leather merchant, then Hayters York Hotel. Next, York Buildings as lodgings or private houses.

(D) A later photograph. Rebuilding has already taken place in York Buildings and, as a horse 'bus waits outside Plummer's, the photograph probably dates from the late 1890s.

Plate 32   **Page 136**

ROBERTSON STREET

A wet afternoon in summer (1890s) and, as always, paving works are in progress. Presumably this was a fête day, Fremlin the brewer having secured a second prize. Despite the weather, quite a number seem to be watching the procession - a free show.

Sadly, the Albert Memorial was finally demolished in 1973, and Plummer's (Debenhams) main Robertson Street premises were rebuilt in the early 1920s.

Many of the shops held their own until the last war. On the right-hand side, briefly (and of most interest), from right to left, Brooker & Jepson's "Book Saloon", later Brooker & Saville, who moved to Trinity Street after the last war, expanded and then failed. Next, Hallett, the watchmaker, later Alcock, and then for many years Hinds, a multiple jeweller; next, what was then the Capital & Counties Bank, in more recent years the local branch of the National Provincial Bank and, after closure following amalgamation with the Westminster Bank, an office of the Leeds Permanent Building Society - the pillared front served both Banks and remained until the Building Society took over. Then follows Brooker & Jepson's, stationers, but for many years the highly regarded H. A. Jepson's store. Then several businesses, most notably Plummer Roddis & Beecroft, later Plummer Roddis and now Debenhams. (In 1894 this firm had a "mourning warehouse" here according to Pike's Directory.)

On the left-hand side, in the distance, The York and York Buildings: to the right of the Memorial are the double-fronted premises of Barker & Rathbone, the china and glassware shop, which became the Electricity Showrooms in the 1930s. Further right, towards Wellington Square, are Messrs. Beck & Jenner, chemists, who were also at Grand Parade.

It is interesting to see reference to two brewers (H. & G. Simonds, and Fremlin & Company). In those days, the 1890s, there was certainly a choice of beers. Pike's Directory for 1894 lists three local breweries:- Hewett of St. Leonards; Burfield, and Breeds, both of Hastings.

In addition, there were local agencies and stores for no less than eight other brewers (mainly Kentish). To a large extent, all had retail outlets in the town - the same Directory shows approximately 150 licensed outlets - choice indeed for a town of less than 60,000 inhabitants.

Plate 33   **Page 137**

THE BRASSEY INSTITUTE, CLAREMONT

(From "The Building News", 6th June 1879).
Erected in 1879 by Thomas Brassey, M. P. for the Borough, later Earl Brassey, and son of the famous railway contractor.

It was built (much as shown) partly as a town residence, and partly to fulfil local needs. It provided, apart from private rooms, a Museum, a Reference Library, and Schools of Art and Science.

In 1887, Lord Brassey, as he had become, presented the building to the town to mark Queen Victoria's Golden Jubilee.

Plate 34   **Page 138**

CAMBRIDGE ROAD

Taken in about 1880 from somewhere near the top of Claremont Steps when this was known as Bohemia Road.

From the left, Noakes, ironmonger, for a long time but, from the mid-1920s, Steele's, newsagents. Next, Beney, furnisher, etc., but from the early 1900s a chemist (Franklin Baird for many years), later a florist, and then a Friendly Society's office. Next, (No. 1 Cambridge Gardens), Saw, bookseller, etc., but from the early 1890s a grocer's shop.

The adjacent private houses were known as Priory Garden Villas, and lasted until the 1930s when most were demolished to make way for the Ritz Cinema. This, in turn, and the remaining houses, then made way for Sainsbury's new premises. Where the shop blinds can be seen was, for many years, Duncan Campbell's Carriage Works, later, in part, Sorrell's Bath Chair Works & Depot and, on the corner of Priory Street, was another grocer. This site was eventually occupied by Skinners Ltd. On the opposite corner of Priory Street, the dimly seen terrace was largely demolished for the G.P.O., erected in the early 1930s.

On the right, with outbuilt porch, is the Tabernacle (originally Calvinistic, but later described as Independent), then the double shopfront of Hy. Lancaster, the furnisher, but from the early 1890s occupied by Plummer Roddis, later Debenhams. Beyond this, and with a square tower, is the Congregational Church built in 1856, replaced in 1885 by the present building, and now known, following amalgamation, as the United Reformed Church.

Finally, a word regarding the gentleman with no qualms about standing in the middle of the road. Victorians dearly loved to have their photograph taken, and presumably this individual realised he was safe as there was relatively little traffic about, unlike today.

Plate 35   **Page 140**

QUEEN'S HOTEL AND ROBERTSON TERRACE

This photograph (note gas street-lighting) was probably taken in the early 1890s and shows the position existing until about 1930.

Until then, all traffic had to go around the Memorial as there was no through road between White Rock Corner and Caroline Place. Harold Place and the beach met without division (just a hump), and there the sailing boats, such as the Albertine, plied for hire: at times of very high water, particularly if this coincided with heavy rainfall, the whole of the Memorial area became an inland sea as in November 1905. The new seafront road and Parade of the 1930s was built out approximately 70 feet seawards and thus straightened the corner at White Rock.

Plate 36   **Page 141**

QUEEN'S HOTEL

This photograph, taken from a different angle than that of Plate 35, does not include Robertson Terrace and must date post-1894 as in that year the whole of the Front from All Saints Street to Grosvenor Gardens was (according to J.M. Baines) lit by electric light. Note electric street lamps. Both Piers clearly visible - a busy scene with much activity.

Plate 32   **ROBERTSON STREET**   Text on Page 134

Ground plan of School of Art

Mr Parsons

Class room

Class room

Corridor

Library

Reading r^m

Bay

Stores

Store

Store

Staircase

Entrance

FEET

THE BRASSEY INSTITUTE, CLAREMONT

CLAREMONT·BVILDINGS·HASTINGS· W. L. VERNON ARCHITECT.

Plate 33   THE BRASSEY INSTITUTE, CLAREMONT   Text on Page 135

Plate 34   **CAMBRIDGE ROAD**   **Text on Page 135**

Plate 37   Page 142

THE ENTRANCE TO THE BATHS,
WHITE ROCK PARADE

This typical mid-Victorian entrance shows the original baths at White Rock Parade, opened in 1874.

The Hastings & St. Leonards Public Baths & Aquarium Company had been formed to carry out an ambitious scheme. The Parade hereabouts was only ten feet wide and the Company therefore built a seaward extension, the roof of which formed a greatly widened promenade, but which in turn accentuated the corner at White Rock, this position existing until a somewhat similar scheme was completed at Carlisle Parade in the early 1930s (see detail for Plate 35). Unfortunately, the subscribed capital of £60,000 was far from adequate and the proposed Aquarium was therefore abandoned and became instead a smaller, separate, ladies' bath. The main bath, 165 feet long, was then, and for many years, the longest bath under cover in the country.

The venture, under-capitalised from the start, was a failure, the mortgagees foreclosed, and after some years of private management and receivership, the Corporation took over a now almost derelict property in 1925. They then embarked on a scheme of reconstruction costing £82,000, giving large and small baths, plus Turkish and medicinal baths, this being one of the many improvement schemes completed between the wars. After nearly another fifty years, the roof was declared dangerous and was replaced by a plastic covering. In 1978 a new Sports Centre, to include a swimming-bath, was planned for the Summerfields Estate - the large bath at White Rock, although still in use, being deemed out of date, and the small bath (unused) being suggested as a suitable site for a skateboarding centre.

A point frequently not realised is the care taken by the Victorians, often considered Philistines to a man, to preserve an amenity - although a public overfed with mass concrete and modern town planning is perhaps becoming more appreciative of this. In the case of the baths, steam power was used originally. Consequently, a chimney was required, and to avoid spoiling the promenade, the builders carried the boiler flues under the road, under the buildings opposite, and into the cliff-face, emerging on the cliff-top.

Plate 38   Page 143

VIEW FROM THE HOSPITAL

This photograph, taken from the old Hospital roof, shows the widened Parade and Baths (see detail for Plate 37), with White Rock on the left and Carlisle Parade plus the Queen's Hotel in the distance. In the foreground is a goat chaise, in the middle of the road a removal van from Gaze & Son (later Gaze, Kane & Company), of the West Marina Pantechnicon, for many years Pickfords Depository. George Gaze of Wellington Square had a finger in many local pies, apart from being the promoter and later director of the Gaiety Theatre of the late 1880s (eventually the Classic Cinema).

Also may be seen the old Bandstand which was moved to White Rock Gardens when these were laid out in the late 1920s - military bands having, for some years, performed in the Parade Extension enclosure completed just before the First World War.

Plate 39   Page 144

THE BATHS

Taken at the same time as Plate 38, but giving more detail.

This clearly shows the separate entrances for ladies and gentlemen, a segregation that extended to the bathing-machines, which were usually labelled (certainly latterly) and were always set apart on the beach. The division continued, for those who wished to change on the spot without cover, until the late 1920s, when separate sections of the beach near Rock-a-Nore, and thus well away from objectors, were still allocated. George Spice (late of the NHS Hastings Executive Council at 21 Claremont) remembered using these beaches with his sister early in the morning (they then both lived in the Old Town).

Mackintosh bathing, popular at this time, was different. In this case, bathers of both sexes journeyed to, and from, the beach wearing their swimming costumes which were covered by mackintoshes (or similar garments). There was no "changing" on the beach, either before or after a swim.

Plate 35   QUEEN'S HOTEL AND ROBERTSON TERRACE   **Text on Page 135**

Plate 36
QUEEN'S HOTEL
Text on Page 135

Plate 37   THE ENTRANCE TO THE BATHS, WHITE ROCK PARADE   **Text on Page 139**

Plate 38

VIEW FROM THE HOSPITAL

Text on Page 139

Plate 39   **THE BATHS**   **Text on Page 139**

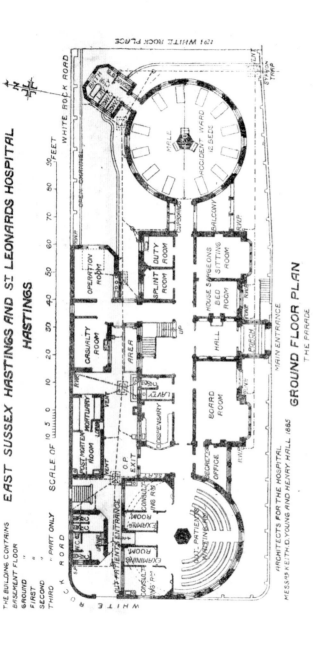

EAST SUSSEX HASTINGS AND ST LEONARDS HOSPITAL
HASTINGS

GROUND FLOOR PLAN
THE PARADE

ARCHITECTS FOR THE HOSPITAL
MESSRS KEITH. D. YOUNG AND HENRY HALL 1885

THE BUILDING CONTAINS
BASEMENT FLOOR
GROUND   "
FIRST   "
SECOND   "
THIRD   "   PART ONLY

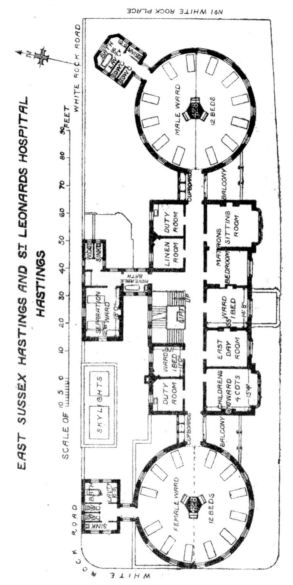

EAST SUSSEX HASTINGS AND ST LEONARDS HOSPITAL
HASTINGS

FIRST FLOOR PLAN
THE PARADE

HOSPITAL PLAN

Text on Page 150

Plate 40

Plate 41   THE HOSPITAL, FROM THE PIER   **Text on Page 150**

Plate 42

THE HOSPITAL

Text on Page 150

Plate 43   **HASTINGS PIER**   Text on Page 150

Plate 44   **HASTINGS PIER**   **Text on Page 150**

Plates 40, 41 and 42 **Pages 145-147**
HOSPITAL PLAN and HOSPITAL
Originally, the Infirmary, built on this site and opened in 1841.
Rebuilt and opened in 1887 opposite the Pier (shown) as the East Sussex Hastings & St. Leonards Hospital, and noted for its circular wards which were, then and for some years, thought superior (see Plan, Plate 40). At the Hastings & St. Leonards Health Congress of 1889, papers on circular wards were submitted by M.K.D. Young, FRIBA, and Dr. Bagshawe of 35 Warrior Square. It is interesting to note that the ward windows were double-glazed to minimise traffic noise!
In 1911, in "Hastings of Bygone Days - And the Present", Cousins wrote, "The present hospital will shortly be removed and a new and up-to-date Institution erected opposite the Sports Ground in Cambridge Road, as a Memorial to the late King Edward VII".
In the event, the new hospital, known as the Royal East Sussex Hospital, and doubling as a War Memorial, was not opened until 1923. The 1887 building was then demolished and on the site was built the White Rock Pavilion - opened by H.R.H. The Prince of Wales in 1927.

Plates 43 and 44 **Pages 148, 149**
HASTINGS PIER
These two early photographs show the Pier in the 1870s as built; a promenade with sea-end pavilion, plus landing stage for pleasure craft, and without intermediate buildings. It was built for the Hastings Pier Company by Laidlaws of Glasgow at a cost of £23,250 from the design of renowned Eugenius Birch, and was opened in 1872 by Earl Granville, then Lord Warden of the Cinque Ports, remembered for his speech in which he referred to "this peerless pier"!
Entrance then cost 2d. which included admission to the pavilion with music or other entertainment. The band played daily in the season, and this must surely have been one of the earliest venues for military bands - the Coldstream Guards are advertised at the toll-gate - note also the separate entrance for bathchairs.

Plate 45 **Page 151**
HAROLD PLACE TO WHITE ROCK
An early print of the slipway at Harold Place, showing the Queen's Hotel as originally built to the designs of F.H. Fowler in 1858/62.
Note the corner pavilions and the original sea side entrance.
A success from the first, the Queen's was quoted ("The Golden Age of British Hotels" - Taylor & Bush) as a Victorian "highflyer" regularly paying 15%, and it continued to prosper until after the Second World War. In recent years the story has been less happy.
In the distance, beyond Carlisle Parade, at the eastern end of White Rock (originally Stratford Place), can be seen the building later occupied by Courts the Furnishers but, for many years, a drapers and costumiers, originally White & Huckell, then White & Norton and, for a short time, Longley's of Bexhill. Further west the Seaside & Pier Hotel, but beyond that the low-built premises of Geo. Gray, wine merchant, this giving way to the original Palace Hotel building of 1886.

Plate 46 **Page 152**
HIGH WATER, EAST OF THE FISHMARKET
This photograph dates probably from the early 1890s.
The sea level would suggest that the harbour works had not commenced, and there is sign neither of the East Hill Lift, nor of the Dust Destructor chimney.
Note the large number of fishing boats.

Plate 47 **Page 152**
FISHING PARTY AT WHITE ROCK
Could this be the start of a fishing competition at White Rock?
We see a number of rowing boats and, of those individuals standing by, quite a number carry rods.

Plate 45   **HAROLD PLACE TO WHITE ROCK**   Text on Page 150

Plate 46   Text on Page 150
**HIGH WATER, EAST OF
THE FISHMARKET**

Plate 47   Text on Page 150
**FISHING PARTY AT
WHITE ROCK**

Plate 48   **Page 154**

THE EASTERN END OF WHITE ROCK PLACE

White Rock Place extended from the Infirmary on the corner of White Rock Road, up to and including the Seaside (later Seaside & Pier) Hotel. Westward was (and is) Verulam Place, eastward to Claremont was then known as Stratford Place, but this for many years has been part of White Rock.

The building with louvred window openings would appear to be part of the White Rock Brewery (1831 - 1885) but, by 1874, it was shown as being occupied by G.G. Gray, wine & spirit merchant.

The Seaside Hotel dated from 1835. In 1881 it became the Seaside & Pier Hotel, but in 1885/86 it was demolished to make way for the second (eastern) portion of the Palace Hotel of 1886, part of the Spiers & Ponds group, the architect being Arthur Wells.

On the cliff behind, the houses of St. Michael's Place where, until the 1890s, was based a secondary Coastguard Station.

Plate 49   **Page 155**

32/33 AND 34 WHITE ROCK

The scene following the demolition of the brewery buildings and the erection of the first (western) portion of the Palace Hotel of 1885.

From the left, the premises of Mr. Walter Stride Addison, the pastrycook and caterer from St. Leonards. Very decorous with a nice Victorian bay and hood, this was No. 32.

Next, Chas. S. Ravenscroft, hairdresser and perfumer, and how delightful to have attention in a "private box". This building is even more pleasing and, although Victorian, retains a touch of Regency style - it is reminiscent of Brighton (Wilds & Busby) or Pennethorne's New Oxford Street, and would look even better if Mr. Ravenscroft refrained from advertising his trade from the rooftop - this is No. 33.

Finally, Gray & Company, now housed in the first of the new Palace Hotel shops at No. 34.

By 1894 Mr. J. Salmon had opened No. 33 as a fancy stationers, and Gray & Company at No. 34 had been replaced by an art dealer.

In 1904, No. 34 was occupied by Arthur Green & Company, hatters and hosiers and, despite changes in ownership, the business continues under the same name today. Here it is interesting to note that the shop front and entrance door shown in the photograph still (1978/79) serve. Later, following the departure of Addison and a subsequent occupant, Salmon took over No. 32 and combined this with No. 33 as Post Office, book and fancy goods shop. It continued in the ownership of the same family until recent years and, although altered externally, a similar business is conducted there today.

Finally, note the goat cart in the foreground. In Victorian days goats were often kept - the Nanny provided milk for the family and the Billy could be used for light delivery work and, perhaps, in summer, to draw a chaise for children, as often seen in seaside towns.

(Compiler's note: The business, Arthur Green & Company, is now closed).

Plate 50   **Page 156**

PALACE HOTEL, SEASIDE & PIER HOTEL, AND 37/38 WHITE ROCK, FORMERLY STRATFORD PLACE

Taken prior to the demolition of the Seaside & Pier Hotel and the building of the eastern extension of the Palace Hotel in 1885/86.

The photograph shows the homeopathic chemist at No. 37 (and if No. 33 was pleasing this is just the reverse). In 1874, Ebenezer Jefferson had been the chemist here and, by 1894, A.E. Bolshaw, who later moved to Claremont. This business was taken over by Mr. S.H. Salmon, Mr. Bolshaw's dispenser, and brother of the bookseller and stationer at 32/33 White Rock. The business continued until the early 1970s but, following the move of Mr. Salmon's son to Lewes, and inability to find a dispenser / manager, this old-established chemist, like so many others, closed down.

In 1874, No. 38 was occupied by W.E. Thorpe, stationer and librarian. Taken over by Markwick, as shown, it had by 1894 become Cima's Swiss Cafe, and continued thus in the hands of the same family until well into the 1930s. In more recent years it was the booking office for the East Kent Road Car Company.

If evidence be needed of the leisurely approach at the time, try to imagine leaving a large packing case in the road there today, even with a boy in charge!

THE EASTERN END OF WHITE ROCK PLACE   Text on Page 153

Plate 48

32/33 AND 34 WHITE ROCK

Plate 49

PALACE HOTEL, SEASIDE & PIER HOTEL, AND   Text on Page 153
37/38 WHITE ROCK, FORMERLY STRATFORD PLACE

Plate 50

Plate 51   Page 158
PALACE PIER, ST. LEONARDS
This Pier, opened in 1891 by Lady Brassey, was built at a cost of some £30,000 to the design of Mr. R. St. G. Moore.

The pavilion was at the shore end and seated 800 people. A greatly advertised facility was that carriages could drive over the Parade and Pier to the very doors!

Later, a sea end pavilion was added and for many years this was used as a roller-skating rink. I remember that, in the company of a bevy of cousins and in an aunt's charge, I saw my first pantomime here in about 1917 - "Aladdin", I think. After the First World War, the pavilion was for a few years the home of the Municipal Orchestra under the conductor, Julian Clifford.

The Pier was never a success and as early as 1894 was in the hands of a Receiver. I have heard that the company was largely financed by the old South-Eastern Railway Company, and even that a cross-Channel link was considered. The railway here, although in a tunnel, is very near the sea, there were excellent hotel facilities and, unlikely as it may seem on this exposed coast, the South-Eastern Railway, under Watkin, did do the most improbable things. Whatever the truth, the Receiver in 1894 was Mr. R.D. Heckels, and his address was South-Eastern Railway Offices, London Bridge Station, S. E.!!

By 1939, and in the years following, the Pier, shabby and lacking in maintenance, suffered further troubles. Cut amidships as a landing precaution, then badly damaged and always at the mercy of the weather, only the sea end pavilion, the home for thousands of gulls, was left and, when this was demolished in 1951, no trace whatsoever remained.

Plate 52   Page 159
MARINA FROM THE PALACE PIER, ST. LEONARDS
This excellent and very detailed photograph must have been taken in the early 1890s.

On the left can be seen the eastern wing of the Royal Victoria Hotel and, in front, a portion of Royal Victoria Buildings - the original baths. Next, the Colonnade, the town's high-class shopping parade, with Messrs. Addison, pastrycooks and caterers, and Messrs. Philpot, the silk mercers, already established some sixty years.

Originally, the shops here were separated from the upper parts, which were purely residential and were approached by entrances at the rear, this to give protection from the weather. Eastward can be seen the impressive (Regents Park style) Marina, including the columnar-faced Craig-y-Don and, at the end, the original Conqueror Hotel which, on the seaward frontage, had columns supporting a pediment.

These fine buildings were all demolished in the 1930s to make way for Marine Court which, for many years, boasted of being the tallest residential building in the Kingdom.

Further east, and on the Parade, is the South Colonnade, again the site of good-class shops and, in its early years, home (at No. 6 or No. 10) of Thomas Campbell, the poet.

Both Victoria Buildings and the South Colonnade were much at the mercy of the sea in rough weather, the latter even having first-floor living accommodation! Both blocks were demolished when the Parade was rebuilt in the late 1930s and the existence of the South Colonnade is recalled by the extreme width of the promenade opposite Undercliff and Marine Court.

Note the lateen sail on the boat in the foreground. This rig is now (1978/79) unknown here, and the gaff rig, once so common, will similarly soon be nothing but a memory.

LEONARD'S PIER.

Plate 51   **PALACE PIER, ST. LEONARDS**   **Text on Page 157**

Plate 52

MARINA FROM THE PALACE PIER, ST. LEONARDS

Text on Page 157

Plate 53   THE ROYAL VICTORIA HOTEL   **Text on Page 161**

THE ROYAL VICTORIA HOTEL

This hotel, first known as the St. Leonards Hotel, was the main building in the new town. The Foundation Stone was laid on 1st March 1828 and it opened for business in October 1829.

Originally, the main entrance was at the rear where it can still be seen, and also initially the hotel did not include the east and west wings, built and used as private houses. Later, the wings were incorporated in the main building and the entrance was moved to the front which was also made more acceptable to mid-Victorian taste as shown in the photograph.

Later still, at the end of the 19th century, the building was almost completely refaced and enlarged, assuming much the appearance it has today, other than for the Tudor Bar, with restaurant above, which was added in the 1930s.

Throughout the Victorian era the hotel was a continued success, and practically everyone of note (other than Queen Victoria) stayed there at some time. In 1849/50 Louis Philippe and Queen Amelie were here following the fall of the Second Empire (see "A Frenchman Sees the English in the Fifties", by Francis Way): further members of the Orleans family stayed at the hotel in 1862, and the Princes Albert and George (later King George V) were on holiday here in 1873. It is said that, in one week in the 1870s, there were twenty dukes and princes in the hotel! In 1887, one of the Rothschilds complained in the Visitors' Book of lack of sunshine in December, and Gladstone was a visitor in 1891.

The original baths (the western pavilion of which is seen) were on the promenade immediately to the front of the hotel and were low built so as not to obscure the view. There were three classical buildings, joined by a screen wall. The eastern housed the Library, Post Office and a branch of the Old Bank; the western was used as the Reading Room; and in the centre was the entrance to the baths. Dorman's Guide (1872) lists six types of bath and also mentions, "A sedan chair is kept on the premises" - I had thought that such conveyances had passed out of use long before. Later, the whole block was converted into shops, these being demolished in the 1930s.

Following the closure, baths were opened in the basement of the Assembly Rooms to the north of the hotel, and a notice can be seen on the side of this building advertising them.

Gausden & Dawson, by the 1890s J.H. Dawson, and later Dawson & Harden, continued as estate agents at Marina until the last war, when they joined up with Mr. C.H. Tanton to form Dawson, Harden & Tanton. Gausden, who came to the town from Hove, where he was one of the promoters of the Sussex County Cricket Ground, was also a "tailor and breeches maker", an example of Victorian "doubling up". This photograph dates from the very early 1890s.

ST. LEONARDS GARDENS

These Gardens, immediately to the north of the Assembly Rooms, were part of James Burton's plan and were formed from a natural wooded valley. They are entered from the South Lodge (a listed building). The differing levels make for pleasing vistas, and the Gardens end near North Lodge (also listed), originally a toll gate. The pond (shown) was a popular spot for mothers with youngsters, as I remember from my own childhood in the early 1900s.

Planned as Subscription Gardens, they continued thus until the merger with Hastings, when they were opened to the public.

There is (1978/79) a small memorial to James Burton, a simple stele with a bronze likeness and a short inscription.

WEST MARINA GARDENS

These Gardens are shown shortly after being laid out by the Corporation.

The fine houses of Grosvenor Gardens date from the late 1880s and originally, in the main, were private or furnished houses. Numbers 1/2, at one time a "Home of Rest", later the Wilton Court Hotel, were, after the last war, converted into flats.

Grosvenor Crescent is yet to be built, but the Bopeep Hotel of 1844, and the entrance to the Brighton Railways West Marina Station, now demolished, can be seen, as well as the railway cottages on the clifftop (West Hill Road).

St. Leonards Gardens. Hastings.

A description of St. Leonards Gardens taken from "The New Stranger's Guide to Hastings & St. Leonards" for 1843

(Note spelling of "skaiters" for "skaters")

The Subscription Gardens at St. Leonards are behind the Assembly Rooms. They were formed by planting and laying out some very uneven ground to the greatest advantage, which has been done so successfully, that after walking about for some time along terraces, by ponds, plantations and summer-houses, you are surprised to detect how small is the base of the whole. The style is rather Swiss. In the Winter the ponds form some remarkably fine ice and are covered with skaiters. There is a scale of prices for keys to the Gardens; a family pays £1.5s. for a year's admission, and 5s. for one week's: with a deposit of 5s. for the key itself, to be returned on its delivery. In these Gardens is preserved a stone called the "Conqueror's Table", which long lay on the site of St. Leonards Hotel, having the reputation of serving that office to William the Conqueror on his invasion; it has been removed here and preserved as an interesting memorial of by-gone times.

(In recent years the "Conqueror's Table" was positioned opposite the Royal Victoria Hotel, formerly known as the St. Leonards Hotel).

Plates 54 and 55   **Text on Page 161**
ST. LEONARDS GARDENS

Plate 56 **WEST MARINA GARDENS** Text on Page 161

Plate 57   **Page 166**

MARINA - 1860/70

This very early photograph is full of interest. Prominently seen is 57 Marina, originally the West Villa and the first house to be constructed in St. Leonards. It was built for James Burton, the developer, and it is said that the structural timbers were brought in by sea. Here it was that the Duchess of Kent and Princess Victoria stayed in the winter of 1834.

Construction was by one of the greatest of the town's earlier builders, "Yorky" Smith, who built largely in the town, and who, it is said, had made money putting up Martello Towers required by Pitt's coastal defence scheme.

After years as a private house (about 100), it became an hotel in the 1930s, and, following war damage, stood empty for many years.

The Marina houses are shown in their original impressive condition, and the Parade seating and the shrubberies are typically mid-Victorian. In the distance, on the extreme left, can be seen a Martello Tower, probably No. 39, stated in 1876 to have collapsed on the seaward side and, shortly after, blown up by the Royal Engineers.

Plate 58   **Page 167**

BOUNDARY ARCH AND GRAND PARADE, ST. LEONARDS

This pleasing picture of St. Leonards Boundary Arch, originally known as East Lodge, was taken in 1886 (according to National Westminster Bank, 1978). It was built by James Burton, the owner-developer of the new town, to mark the eastern boundary of St. Leonards, and lasted until 1895 when, due to divided opinion regarding its proposed removal, the Borough Council took speedy action and demolished it completely in seven hours on the night of 22nd January. J.M. Baines (in "Burton's St. Leonards") states that objection on the part of ratepayers was not so much due to sentiment as to wrath at a proposed charge of £1,700 for road widening!!

The southern pedestrian arch was never open, and originally provided a room for the St. Leonards beadle, Harmer, who operated from 1832/36, when the Hastings Borough Police Force was formed and

took over his duties. Later it became a shop, in its last years occupied by a bootmaker.

Immediately behind can be seen the single-storey building of two rooms which was the office and meeting-place of the St. Leonards Commissioners from the mid-1860s until the final amalgamation with Hastings. It then became in turn, a rates office, veterinary surgeon's premises, estate agent's office and, in the post-war years, a taxi call office. To the right can be seen (at 3/4 Grand Parade) what became the National Westminster Bank, the building then in course of construction. Opened in 1886 by the London & County Bank, it was probably the first breaching of the formal St. Leonards terraces and, unlike its neighbours, is, therefore, very much late Victorian.

On the western corner of London Road can be seen the once popular Royal Saxon Hotel.

Note the kerbside railing, giving protection from traffic, but no protection whatsoever on the sea side.

Plates 59 and 60   **Pages 168, 169**

VERULAM PLACE, GRAND HOTEL, AND EVERSFIELD PLACE

Verulam Place is a very short section of the seafront extending from 67 Eversfield Place to White Rock Road. In Pike's Directory for 1876, eleven individual tenants are shown but, by 1894, there were great changes.

The Grand Hotel now appears flanked on each side by shops with upper parts. The hotel was financed by a locally promoted company, and was probably built in the 1880s. Pike, for 1894, shows, "Grand Hotel, Restaurant and Buffet, Chas. Reinmann, Manager, Tèle. 68". However, its life as an hotel was short and, by 1915, it had become residential flats (Regency Mansions) and, by 1935, two blocks, Waverley Court and Regency Mansions. Two buildings still remained on either side (the most easterly the newly-built Borough Information Bureau) and, up to the Second World War, the Grand Restaurant continued its independent existence. By the 1960s, the whole block (except for the Information Bureau) had been demolished - a luxury skyscraper hotel was planned but, perhaps fortunately, succumbed to one of the many post-war financial crises.

On Plate 59 will be seen the premises of H.M. Baker, grocer & estate agent - this business lasted as agents until 1939. In Victorian days, grocers and estate agents often doubled (Baker did the same in Tunbridge Wells) and, in Hastings & St. Leonards, Cave Austin & Company had an agency at Grand Parade (later taken over by H. Tanton). Mayor Revill also conducted a similar dual business at Wellington Place.

Note also in Plate 59 a plentiful showing of growlers and bath-chairs, and what appears to be a horse 'bus, and, in Plate 60, a hansom cab - something I never remember in Hastings.

Plates 61, 62 and 63   Page 170
EAST OF THE ARCHWAY

Plate 61   Page 170
THE SLIPWAY AT WARRIOR SQUARE

This existed until the 1930s when the Parade was rebuilt in its present form. There were always plenty of small boats here, and these were brought on to the Parade at times of bad weather. The print is quite early in date, and one wonders if the boathook and box represent early life-saving equipment. The slipway was also used by carters to collect goods brought in by sea and this practice must have continued well into the 1870s as my aunt, M.A. Morris (born 1868), could remember coal being unloaded here.

In the distance can be seen the Archway and the impressive eastern front of the Conqueror Hotel, this fine building, reminiscent of Regents Park, being the first house of the Burton marine terraces. Also clearly seen is the large, three-storey, bow to Adelaide House, once a winter house for Queen Adelaide. Here, for many years, was a branch of Ellis Son and Vidler. Nearer, on the south-west corner of Warrior Square, stands the building which preceded the late Victorian Clubhouse of the East Sussex Club.

Plate 62   Page 170
WARRIOR SQUARE AND EVERSFIELD PLACE

On the eastern corner of the Square, the premises of E.H. Hasselby, chemist, (in 1875 Messrs. Hasselby & Robinson) can be seen. At the turn of the 20th century the premises became a branch of the London & South Western Bank, and continued as Barclays Bank. It is noteworthy that, for well over 100 years, there was a gentlemen's outfitters here, originally Moppett, and then trading as Jefferies. Referring to chemists, it is interesting to note how many pharmacists the town once supported.

Pike	1894 shows	42	including	5 company shops
Pike	1915	34		2
Pike	1937	35		4
Pike	1958	30		3
Yellow Pages	1978	16		3

The number in earlier days was, no doubt, due in part to the numerous visiting invalids endeavouring to regain their health. Economic causes (in common with other parts of the country) resulted in the sadly reduced number in 1978. In the town centre here I can remember 7 or 8 good, independent chemists.

Plate 63   Page 170
THE JUMBO ROCKS

This is a very early and interesting photograph, dating from before 1866, as the Commissioners' office adjacent to the Archway is not shown.

The terrace (originally Adelaide Place), but later included in Grand Parade and extending from Market Street to London Road, is shown in more or less its original state and before the building of the London & County Bank.

At the western end, originally, the Harold Hotel opened in December 1830, by Henry Edlin: at the eastern end the more successful South Saxon Hotel, licensed in 1832 by William Eldridge and, from the beginning, an important coaching house. Further east, and beyond London Road, can be seen the huge bow of Adelaide House and the south-western corner of Warrior Square.

Plate 57

MARINA - 1860/70

Text on Page 164

Plate 58   **BOUNDARY ARCH AND GRAND PARADE, ST. LEONARDS**   **Text on Page 164**

Plate 59   **VERULAM PLACE, GRAND HOTEL, AND EVERSFIELD PLACE**   **Text on Page 164**

Plate 60 **VERULAM PLACE, GRAND HOTEL, AND EVERSFIELD PLACE** **Text on Page 164**

Plate 61 *Above:* The slipway at Warrior Square

Plate 62 *Above right:* Warrior Square and Eversfield Place

Plate 63 *Below right:* The Jumbo Rocks

Plate 64 WARRIOR SQUARE **Text on Page 174**

Plate 65   **WARRIOR SQUARE**   **Text on Page 174**

Plate 66

WARRIOR SQUARE

Text on Page 174

WARRIOR SQUARE

This Square, the only real opening on the seafront, was commenced on the eastern side in the 1850s and completed in 1864. It was developed by James Troup. Said by some to be the largest Square in England, in its original state of near one hundred almost identical six-floor houses it was an impressive development.

At the rear of the gardens can be seen Warrior Square Terrace. These houses, in some cases even larger, were, in at least one case, still privately occupied up to the early 1930s, Miss Bethune-Eversfield (of Denne Park, Horsham) keeping No. 1 as a marine residence for occasional use and thus maintaining the family connection.

The originally private gardens were, in later years, owned by Major Holman of the Warrior House and Edinburgh House Hotels and the founder of Dowling & Company, auctioneers and estate agents. The town acquired the gardens in sections, Major Holman finally donating the upper part in 1930. Sadly, during the Second World War, the Square suffered severely.

WARRIOR SQUARE

These two photographs show the eastern side of the Square built 1853/64, with Plate 65 showing a part of Warrior Square Terrace and, in the distance, Warrior Gardens.

Although lacking the character of earlier development to the west, the sheer size of the Square, each property with similar canted bays, is, like it or not, impressive.

The photographs both date from the so-called "palmy" days, when coal could be had for twenty shillings a ton and when enough servants to run these six-floor houses would mean a wage bill of little more than £100 per annum.

The corner property in Plate 66 was, as the discreet wall sign states, the Warrior House Hotel. This continued for over 100 years but with varying fortune, finally being known as the Warrior Hotel. From the first, many of these large properties were used as lodging

houses but, at the same time, there were many wealthy residents. In the 1870s, when the Borough still returned two Members of Parliament, both Thomas Brassey and Kay Shuttleworth maintained houses in the Square, and this continued in the 1880s when Wilson Noble lived at No. 43.

THE ST. LEONARDS BANK

This photograph, probably taken in the 1880s, shows the St. Leonards branch of Beechings Bank, the first fully staffed bank in St. Leonards, although the Old Bank had conducted an agency at Southalls Library for many years before. (See detail for Plate 53). On the right the fairly new-built premises of the St. Leonards & East Sussex Club and, on the left, Messrs. Beck & Jenner, one of the many chemists. Beechings was eventually taken over by Lloyds Bank, as explained below.

Banking in Hastings started in about 1791, (see detail for Plates 5 and 6), when it was reported that Messrs. Tilden, Shadwell, Hilder, Harvey & Gill were "proving of benefit to visitors". According to the first Hastings Guide (Stell's) of 1794, "The summer visitants are now at no loss to get their drafts discounted". Gill was the town clockmaker, and the Bank operated from his home at 90 High Street, opposite The Roebuck. He was the father-in-law of William Scrivens, the elder, whose son, George (born 1807) joined the Bank in 1832, becoming a partner about 1840, the Bank thereafter being known as Smith, Hilder, Scrivens & Company. A branch was already in being at St. Leonards and, by 1856, the Bank had moved to Pelham Place (see detail for Plate 23).

Despite competition, the business prospered and opened further branches but, unfortunately, in 1857, it failed for £150,000. A petition for bankruptcy was lodged against the partners and at the enquiry it was revealed that the failure was mainly due to large advances having been made to a farmer who was related to a partner - I have heard that the trouble was hops! James Hilder, in his eighties, who was primarily responsible, proved obstructive in every way. One of his ledgers had been destroyed and his examination had to be repeatedly deferred. Had there been more co-operation, the failure could probably have been avoided as, ultimately, all debts were paid in full, and first-class certificates were given to George Scrivens and Francis Smith. The first-named was held in the highest esteem by the townspeople (this fact confirmed by my grandmother, Ann Morris), and a presentation of silver was made as a mark of public regard. At the time, Commissioner Fane said of George Scrivens (in "The Spectator" of 26th December 1857), "He has ended a most honourable career with the stigma of bankruptcy, owing to the less correct conduct of his partners. He has led a life of honesty, integrity and economy and, as regards his private affairs, he does not owe one farthing".

This high regard was emphasised when, in 1859, Messrs. Beeching, Hodgkin & Beeching of Tunbridge Wells, opened a branch at Pelham Place under the managership of George Scrivens and, later, branches were opened at St. Leonards (shown here) and Bexhill. The Hastings office was subsequently moved to Wellington Place, where it continues today. Beechings (in trouble) was taken over by Lloyds in 1890, but the Wellington Place Branch is (or perhaps one should say was) always thought of as the Old Bank. George Scrivens, as Manager, was the town's first Treasurer, legally then permissible, and, in the past, all Borough accounts were held by Lloyds, Hastings.

Plate 68 **Page 177**
HOLLINGTON CHURCH-IN-THE-WOOD
Dedicated to either St. Rumbold or St. Leonard, and on which Dr. Bullock, despite sixteen pages in his history of The Church-in-the-Wood, Hollington, of 1949, gives no firm ruling.

The church may well be of Saxon origin, but no definite evidence is available. Neither is there any reference in the Domesday Book, but there is documentary evidence that the "Chapel of Hollington" was in existence in 1090. Until the late 18th, or early 19th, century, the church continued to serve its isolated rural community with only few visits by strangers. By the 1790s, however, Hastings was beginning to attract visitors and, from 1794, the date of the first Guide Book (Stell's), constant references to the church were made in the various Guides published almost every year and, consequently, it became the subject of an excursion for most visitors.

With Hastings at this time attracting practically every artist of note, and with most writers also paying visits, the church was now more frequented. It was a favourite excursion for Charles Lamb, and figures often in his letters. Despite disparaging remarks in his essay, "The Old Margate Hoy", later correspondence contains many flattering references to the church, and to Hastings and its surroundings.

By mid to late Victorian days, the church became popular and had a wealthy congregation. Bequests and donations meant alterations and restoration. As with Fairlight, it became a favourite burial place for the rich. From 1900 Great-Uncle George H. Brett was Parish Clerk, and this most definitely proved no drawback to his Monumental Mason's business, strategically sited at Baldslow, midway between the Borough Cemetery and the Church-in-the-Wood.

Plates 69 and 70 **Pages 178, 179**
ST. JOHN'S, UPPER ST. LEONARDS
These two prints show the exterior and interior of the third church, built 1881/84.

Few parishes anywhere can have built four churches in less than 100 years, but the congregation here had to do just that. In the early 1860s, a fast-growing, wealthy population had no churches nearer than St. Leonards Parish Church or St. Mary Magdalen.

The first Christ Church had just been consecrated, and the Reverend C.L. Vaughan (the first Rector there) was largely responsible for the proposed St. John's. In 1865, a temporary iron church was erected, but this was destroyed by a gale. In July 1867, a brick-built church was opened, but this burnt down in 1878. In July 1881, the third St. John's (Architect Sir Arthur Blomfield) was consecrated, this being the building shown in the photographs. This was destroyed (except for the tower) by enemy action in 1943 and, in 1951/57, the present church (Architect Goodhart-Rendell) was built.

THE ST. LEONARDS BANK

Plate 67

Plate 68   **HOLLINGTON CHURCH-IN-THE-WOOD**   **Text on Page 175**

Plate 69 ST. JOHN'S, UPPER ST. LEONARDS **Text on Page 175**

Plate 70 ST. JOHN'S, UPPER ST. LEONARDS **Text on Page 175**

Plate 71　　　　　　　　**GENSING GARDENS LOOKING NORTH-EAST**　　　　　　　　**Text on Page 183**

Plate 72 **GENSING GARDENS LOOKING SOUTH-EAST** **Text on Page 183**

Plate 73   **HASTINGS STATION**   **Text on Page 183**

Plate 71   **Page 180**

GENSING GARDENS LOOKING NORTH-EAST

Anglesea Terrace to the left, London Road in the middle distance and, near the skyline, the red-brick St. Peter's, Bohemia, by James Brooks and dating from 1885. Note the cast-iron framed seats shown.

According to Pike's Directory (1894) the Gardens:-

"Are well laid-out and kept in order for lawn tennis and croquet parties."

Judging from the dress of the "young ladies and gentlemen" pictured, who are behaving with proper decorum, the photograph could date from the very late 1890s.

Plate 72   **Page 181**

GENSING GARDENS LOOKING SOUTH-EAST

This shows the pond and, through the trees, London Road.

According to "The Homeland Booklet", 1901:-

"These are very pleasant grounds and are tastefully laid-out with carpet flower beds, lawns and pond with wild fowl, seats and shady nooks and grounds for lawn tennis."

As with the previous view of Gensing Gardens, Plate 71, this could also date from the very late 1890s.

Plate 73   **Page 182**

HASTINGS STATION

An arrival at a very early date, and a photograph of great interest to any student of railway history.

Note the four-wheeled carriages with "pot" lamps, what appears to be the very old type of padded buffer, an early guard's birdcage lookout and, most interesting of all, the private carriage brought down by rail.

Measom's S. E. Railway Guide of 1863, quoting the general regulations, states:-

"Passengers travelling in private carriages (not being servants) are required to take first-class tickets; such passengers may remove during the journey to the Company's first-class carriages *if there be room for them.*"!

The solitary porter does not appear to be lacking work, and let us hope the passengers were suitably generous.

At the time of the photograph, the station would have consisted of just one long platform. Some time prior to 1899 (when reconstruction was considered) a bay platform was added. Subsequently, a further bay was built, and the station continued unchanged until a new building was opened on 6th July 1931.

Plates 74, 75, 76 and 77   **Pages 184 - 186**

ST. MARY STAR OF THE SEA CHURCH, HIGH STREET

(Plan and artist's impressions from "The Builder", 27th August 1887)

The church was built at the expense of the Victorian poet, Coventry Patmore, in memory of his second wife.

Professor Pevsner, in "Sussex" - 1965 - "The Buildings of England", is unusually enthusiastic. In his general introduction he says, "The Victorian church of Hastings which everyone will remember is St. Mary Star of the Sea by Champneys (1882)". (As mentioned within the textual detail for Plate 14, according to Derek Patmore, "Portrait of my Family", 1935, it was completed in 1883). Pevsner adds, "Best in the town", and, when describing the building: "Impressive inside and out".

Patmore, who from 1875 to 1891 lived at Old Hastings House, the former home of the Milwards (then known as "The Mansion") had admired the property as a small boy when visiting the town in the late 1820s. He had hoped to end his days in Hastings but, when 68 years of age, ownership of the property changed and, following a dispute with the new owner, he had to leave and moved to Lymington, Hampshire.

————◄o►————

The Plan

Saint Mary·Star·of the Sea Hastings

Basil Champneys B.A
Architect

The South-west Aspect

Plates 74 and 75   **ST. MARY STAR OF THE SEA CHURCH, HIGH STREET**   **Text on Page 183**
Plan and South-West Aspect, taken from "The Builder", 27th August 1887.

The North-East Aspect

Plate 76   **ST. MARY STAR OF THE SEA CHURCH, HIGH STREET**   **Text on Page 183**

North-East Aspect, taken from "The Builder", 27th August 1887.

View looking East

ST. MARY STAR OF THE SEA CHURCH, HIGH STREET Text on Page 183

View looking East, taken from "The Builder", 27th August 1887.

Plate 77

⌐∘ঔ Appendix ঔ∘⌐

Books, Book-Binders and Bookcases

Originally intended for publication in mid-October 2008, *Hurrah for Hastings! A Celebration*, has been delayed due to circumstances beyond my control. Eagle-eyed observers of the town's fortunes will note that, since penning *Jottings*, the long-established firm of *Arthur Green*, gentlemen's outfitters, has closed, and much-respected *Howes Bookshop* is now conducting its business from P.O. Box No. 327, Hastings, and not from *Trinity Hall*, Braybrooke Terrace.

The present economic downturn has been brought about by massive greed and complete lack of financial control. The abandonment of the mutuality principle by certain building societies has also played a not inconsiderable part in contributing to this country's present sorry state. Both my father, of the old-style *Halifax Building Society*, and George Scrivens, of *The Hastings Old Bank*, would have been particularly appalled by the current position. In time it will be interesting to see whether or not there is a (forced) reversion to simpler ways. Will there be a return to "old-fashioned" values, along with skills such as home baking and cooking, using seasonal, locally-grown produce? Will there be a reduction in planned obsolescence and a cutting-back of excessive packaging? And will we be content with down-to-earth pleasures and holidays close to home? I wonder - time will tell ....

As a member of the *Old Hastings Preservation Society*, on 15th October 2008 I spoke at *The History House* on "Books, Book-Binders and Bookcases". The title of the talk was appropriate in my opinion as books have meant much to different generations and branches of my family - indeed, as mentioned elsewhere, the first Hastings Scrivens, William, innkeeper of the famous *Swan Coaching Inn*, was one of four proprietors of the first circulating library which opened initially in Croft Road in 1788 with a stock of just over 1,500 volumes. In my father's collection was a copy of Lady Brassey's *In the Trades, the Tropics, and the Roaring Forties*, this having been personally inscribed and presented by her in 1884 to Edward H. Marshall, M.A., the first librarian at the Free Reference Library, Claremont, established in 1881. He would have been known to the Brasseys as, at that time, they maintained a private suite at *The Institute*.

Items such as W. G. Moss's 1824 *History & Antiquities of Hastings*; James Rouse's 1825 volumes on the County of Sussex; the complete (1926/56, with Index) *Sussex County Magazine*; and W. D. Cooper's 1853 *Glossary of Sussex Provincialisms* sat happily alongside Charles Fleet's 1882/1883 volumes, *Glimpses of our Sussex Ancestors*, with other treasures, many acquired gradually over years of pleasurable bookshop investigation.

I also covered the subject of Craft Book-Binders and their links to Hastings. Until approximately the 1920s, my family had very close ties to the Haydays, much-respected Victorian Craft Book-Binders, John Hayday and his wife, Ann, having retired to St. Leonards in the late 1880s. Book-Binders to the House of Lords, the firm was much favoured by publisher William Pickering, who established his business in London in 1820 and was particularly concerned with the appearance of his books. He was noted for publishing special editions covering the English Poets. Many of Ruskin's later works are in Hayday bindings, too. The Haydays were renowned for the finish and the gilding of their bindings, these still being much sought-after by specialist collectors. I am fortunate enough to have examples at home which show their skilled craftsmanship, together with a number of Ann's personal possessions, and her photograph. Originally from Edinburgh, she was particularly close to my great-aunt Nell and, when Ann was widowed, she moved to join Nell in my great-grandparents' home in Silverhill. Ann Hayday was noted for her generosity and lived to a very great age. Every Sunday the vicar of *St. Matthew's Church*, Silverhill, visited her personally at home to give Holy Communion and, every Sunday, the vicar departed with the gift of one guinea (21 shillings), a lot of money in the early years of the last century. Not surprisingly, my family was not best pleased when, returning home from Mrs. Hayday's funeral, it was discovered that the vicar's account in respect of attendance at the proceedings had already been delivered. It was felt to be in rather poor taste, particularly in view of the close connection with *St. Matthew's Church*. Although my great-grandparents had been married at *St. Mary-in-the-Castle Church* in the 1860s, they lived in Silverhill for many years and *St. Matthew's* featured prominently in their lives, too, and in the lives of their children. (Mrs. Hayday is mentioned briefly within Thomas Scrivens's First World War letter home, an extract from which appears on Page 22 of this book).

I took along to *The History House* a copy of Ruari McLean's 1974 book on Victorian Book-Bindings which contains a number of examples of the Hayday skills. Many Victorian bindings are breathtakingly beautiful, and another link to Hastings in this regard comes with the Zaehnsdorf family, the founder of the firm being Joseph Zaehnsdorf, an immigrant to this country in the early 1800s from what is now Budapest. The last member of the firm, Ernest, retired to Hastings (Fairlight, I believe) from Watford in 1947. He was a director of the London-based company until 1957, dying in 1970 at the age of 90. I also had with me Frank Broomhead's 1966 book on the Zaehnsdorfs which again gives examples of their craft, and I am lucky to have some of their bindings at home as well.

As will be realised from reading my personal reminiscences, (Page 68), books have meant a great deal to me from early childhood - hence my written recollections of so many local dealers whom (through my father) I came to know. I remember that the subject of bookcases was a frequent topic of conversation in our household - after all, the ever-growing collection (not relating solely to Hastings and Sussex) had, somehow, to be accommodated. As books continued to arrive, so too did shelving and different types of bookcase - all still with me, plus additions.

Leonard Scrivens and daughter, Cynthia, on a happy and hot summer's afternoon in 1967 in Warrior Square Gardens, St. Leonards. These Gardens were originally in private ownership - see text detail for Plate 64.

On 15th October 2008 I showed some unusual Hastings items, such as the interesting Poll Book of the Hastings Election for 1868, (Mayor William Scrivens being the Returning Officer), this copy having belonged to George Meadows, Town Clerk at the time, and also the lush 1933 Hastings & St. Leonards Gas Company Centenary publication, full of photographic detail. A few seaside-related ephemera pieces were taken along, too. As the previous day had been the 14th October, the most significant date in English history (this day in 1066 being the last time we were defeated on home soil) I quoted an extract from the 1896 book *On Southern English Roads* by topographical writer and illustrator, James John Hissey. As readers may know, this book was one of a series of fourteen volumes, these in style being somewhat reminiscent of C.G. Harper's famous *Road* books, but starting in 1884, earlier than Harper. (Both writers featured prominently on my father's shelves). The extract in question is reproduced below:

"Glancing southwards and seawards, the fine rounded sweep of Pevensey Bay (where the war-like Normans landed of old) came into view, with the many Martello Towers marshalled in orderly array along its shore, the white foam of the breaking waves being traceable far, far away in curving parallels with the pebbly beach: and beyond the Bay, hazily indistinct, could just be discerned the bold cliffs above Hastings, the town itself being half-hidden by a blue veil of its own smoke. We called a short halt to enjoy the wide panorama of land and sea. Through our field-glasses we could make out Pevensey's ruined castle, a dark spot in the sun-steeped landscape, and the uplands by Battle where the Normans won them a kingdom: we looked upon historic ground!"

I also quoted from Sheila Kaye-Smith's well-known atmospheric novel *Tamarisk Town*, published in 1919, relating to Marlingate, in reality, of course, Hastings. This piece, too, being relevant, is shown here:

"The dusk hung over the sea and streets - a web in which were meshed dim orange stars, the lights of house windows and little shops, and the lights of the fishing-boats that bobbed on the deep waters off Rock-a-Nore."

The earliest item I had with me was the first *Hastings Guide*, published in 1794 by Stell, which (as I said) promoted Hastings excellently, the new town of St. Leonards not being developed until 1828 by James Burton. Hastings was starting to attract visitors and Stell, within his *Guide*, gave the town admirable publicity, drawing attention to its many advantages. "Great oaks from little acorns grow" and that was certainly the case following on from the 1794 *Guide*. With the ever-increasing popularity of the town, coupled with the ever-growing population, as the years passed the area became awash with Guide-book type publications. Stell certainly set the ball rolling and, by the 1890s, the initial trickle of advertisements within these books concerning Hastings (and St. Leonards) had developed into a torrent, all of them providing a fascinating insight into the lives of our forebears. As my father wrote, succinctly, 30 years ago, in the foreword to his notes, "At the turn of the 20th century, Hastings, with St. Leonards, was the second largest seaside resort in the U. K., second only to Brighton", this certainly a point worthy of particular note. All tradesmen were anxious to promote their wares to the general public. Of course, the development of the Railway Age meant that travel was becoming much easier, this playing a considerable part in the fortunes of Hastings and St. Leonards.

From 1821, the *5th Guide* includes a special reference to the *Castle Hotel* in Wellington Square, the hotel being opened originally in 1818. The *Guide* states that it is "situated in the centre of new buildings: it is a very handsome house and commands an exceeding good view of the sea and country in the vicinity. From Mr. Emary the visitants meet with the very best accommodation. The airy cheerfulness of the situation is particularly noticed by strangers". I, too, remember its "airy cheerfulness", but from childhood in 1962 - not 1821! (See Pages 75 and 89).

In 1841, widely travelled and highly judgemental Dr. A.B. Granville, (1783-1872), writing in the third volume of his *Spas of England*, naturally covers Hastings and St. Leonards separately. He is concerned with accommodation from a delicate invalid's point of view and, referring to the highly-important coaching inn, *The Swan*, expresses the rather sour opinion that, "Assuredly no invalid would think of sojourning in so dull a neighbourhood"! He describes the trials and tribulations of seeking out accommodation and is constantly worried about invalids' exposure to the elements. He is also concerned about a patient's need to become accustomed to the incessant roaring as he/she "will be on the margin of a too frequently agitated ocean". Finally, Dr. Granville plumps for *The Albion* in the summer and *The Marine Hotel* in the winter. Writing at length about St. Leonards, again he complains about exposure to the elements, but considers that behind *The Marina* and near to *The Assembly Rooms* "the whole varied region is a little paradise to invalids". Summing up, Dr. Granville prefers, from a medical point of view, inland Spas. What would he have made of *The Good Girl's Present* from 1840, I wonder? This child's book (with engravings) features the highly fashionable seaside and details how the sea-breezes helped a young invalid. Furthermore, Frederick Stockdale, within his *Sketches* from 1817, had nothing but praise for Hastings. The town restored his health and he said, flatteringly, "I never enjoyed more ample scope for my pencil".

From *The New Stranger's Guide* of 1843 we learn that "The South-Eastern or Dover Railroad is now completed as far as Staplehurst, being only a distance of 22 miles from Hastings. There are Stations at Tunbridge and Staplehurst, from which Coaches run several times during the day to and from Hastings and St. Leonards". Also provided are interesting snippets such as the fact that Mr. Hore, being the local Cupper, is available to bleed individuals as and when required, and that women seldom, if ever, go pandling here - in other words, shrimping.

George Measom's *Official Illustrated Guide to the South-Eastern and North and mid-Kent Railways*, from 1863, naturally features Hastings and St. Leonards. Aside from interesting advertisements for local firms, on Page 252 there is a description of the fishing population, together with an outline of a Dutch Auction. "The fish are shot out on the beach, and the seller begins the bidding at a very high figure which he lowers by degrees, until the price becomes marketable. The first person who catches his eye and shouts 'Snaps!' becomes the purchaser of the lot, which is immediately transferred to the railway and reaches Midland towns in the course of a few hours". This *Guide* has a special section on the commercial aspect of Hastings, together with good engravings, and great attention is paid to the *Patent Carriage Works* of Messrs. Rock & Son, White Rock, and Baker Street West, London, by appointment to H. M. The Queen. At the *Great Exhibition* of 1851 they exhibited their well-known *Dioropha* or two-headed Carriage for which they received the Prize Medal. They then exhibited Carriages at the *Paris Universal Exhibition* in 1855, again winning the Medal and many commendatory remarks. They continued winning awards at the *International Exhibition* of 1862, becoming extremely eminent in their field. Apparently the *Dioropha* could be made in any style and of any size, from that of the miniature brougham to the largest family coach. Finally, we are told that, "All prejudices in favour of the London Marts will be dissipated before the visitor has been halfway through these premises". A splendid full page engraving appears within Measom's Guide, complete with a curious dog! Of course, it must be remembered that this was a time when the horse was all-important.

Of the same era, Francis Frith, one of the great pioneer photographers of the mid-Victorian age, produced excellent images of the town within *The Gossiping Photographer at Hastings* from 1864 - very early for a book of this type. The frontispiece is reproduced at the end of this Appendix.

The outside back cover of the informative first *Butcher, Cole & Company* Directory for 1874-75 features a gilded advertisement for John Bray of 13 Marina, South Colonnade, St. Leonards. Described as a "House and Estate Agent", other business interests included acting as a "Wine, Spirit and Beer Merchant" and as an Agent for Salt & Company, Brewers, Burton-on-Trent. Within the Directory are good advertisements, including a full page devoted to Alfred Duke (from an Old Town family) then in business as a "Hatter, Hosier and Shirtmaker", opposite the Albert Memorial. Alfred's brother, Samuel, was manager of the *Trade Protection Society*, then in Wellington Place. The Duke family was continually and closely connected with the *T.P.S.* (as it was known) which, in time, moved to Claremont. I remember the *Society* from my very early working days in the late 1960s, and recall Mrs. Duke, too.

By the time we reach 1876, we find that the *Pike & Ivimy Directory* is full of intriguing advertisements such as that for William Keen, General & Furnishing Ironmonger of 23 Robertson Street. A full list of items available is given, such as perambulators; iron and brass bedsteads; gas chandeliers, in glass, bronze and ormolu; coal vases and scoops (newest designs); garden seats and chairs; mangles; and, most notably, washing machines. These latter were <u>very</u> early in date. The handful of manufacturers producing them in the 19th century sold them to the owners of mansions, large country houses, hotels, schools, and commercial laundries. At home I have, still in excellent working condition, a thermometer bought by my great-grandmother from this shop, perhaps at the time the *Directory* was issued. It is stamped up with the detail "William Keen, Hastings", and is a solid wooden object with metallic fittings.

Extending Victorian panoramas saw the light of day, too, on 15th October as they provide a good, visual idea of the appearance at that time of Hastings and St. Leonards. Also receiving an "airing" were a couple of early Victorian humorous seaside panoramas.

On the subject of humour, special mention must be made of Queen Victoria's drawing master, Edward Lear (1812 - 1888), whose "Jumblies" 'nonsense' verses I recall reciting as a very small child at the time of the annual Hastings Musical Festival. Many of Lear's writings (not his rhymes of four lines) have a touching, melancholic streak - strangely comforting at difficult times. Lear had connections with members of the Pre-Raphaelite Movement and, in common with them, he had strong, affectionate ties to Hastings, enjoying the fresh air and making good use of the local scenery as inspiration for several of his paintings. On a completely different note, the quirky "Sammy's Bed", from 1857, tells, by way of illustrations, the sorry tale of an uncomfortable night's sleep at St. Leonards in too short a bed!

Many famous authors and writers have had connections with Hastings and St. Leonards - far too many to discuss here. In their way, children's books linked to the seaside provide us with much social history detail from a child's perspective, the seaside playing an important part in the lives of many - not all, by any means, but a great number, nevertheless. The name of Harry Furniss is well-known in the area. Born in 1854 and dying in 1925, he lived for a long time at East Cliff House, moving after 1914 to 8 High Wickham. He had many strings to his bow, such as working in the Film Industry with Thomas Edison, and was also a pioneer, in 1914, of the animated cartoon. He wrote many books, but is probably best known as an artist and illustrator, notably with *Punch* magazine, and he illustrated special editions of works by Carroll, Dickens and Thackeray. In 1886 he illustrated an extremely charming children's book entitled *Romps*, which I think is of equal appeal to adults. The illustrations, in colour and black and white, cover four different "Romps", including *Romps at the Seaside*. In a nutshell, this shows children enjoying themselves in different ways, appropriate to the era, and having unabashed good fun by the sea!

Hastings Trolley-bus BDY 777 (Maidstone & District) pictured in May 1959 on East Parade, Old Town. During that year trolley-buses were replaced by the powerful Atlantean buses. On the side of the trolley-bus is an advertisement for "Longley's Department Store" of Devonshire Road, Bexhill, and (for a short time) of White Rock, Hastings. (The compiler remembers, when small, being taken to see Father Christmas at the Bexhill store, and also participating, at Devonshire Road, in a children's "fashion show" in aid of charity, c. 1955/56). On left of card is detail for "The Cutter", advertising restaurant facilities, availability of accommodation, and stating "Visitors Welcome", all beneath an illustration of, naturally, a cutter.

Aunt Louisa's Book of the Seaside, from 1867, covers seaside activities of an earlier time by way of simple words and Kronheim illustrations (a printing process involving oil colours, not ink). *Launch the Lifeboat!*, from the 1890s, is exactly what it purports to be, namely, it covers the launch of a lifeboat from that era (with cork lifejackets, etc.) and is again well-illustrated and aimed at children. *The Seaside Holiday Alphabet* from the turn of the 20th century, colourful and entertaining, shows fun and games.

As well as enjoying themselves, Victorian children (and adults) <u>learned</u> a great deal at the seaside, being fascinated by the wonders of the deep and of the seashore, this particular fascination actually pre-dating the Victorian era very considerably. From 1869, *Walter at the Seaside - Facts and Fancies about the Shore and the Deep*, has a dramatic frontispiece, *A Narrow Escape*. Aimed at youngsters, the book is packed with clear engravings and educational features. Children were encouraged to collect specimens for their sea-water aquaria at home and *The Little Folks Annual* of 1880 has an article on this subject, along with engravings. Pike's *Guide* from that era has a feature (and a detailed half-page engraving) on *The Seaweed Shop* in Trinity Street, Hastings. Seaweed decorations were made for the table, and drawing-room ornaments were produced, as well as "yacht" decorations which were, apparently, "simply invaluable". The windows of the shop are crammed with shells of all types. The subject of the seaside (and shells) featured prominently on Victorian Christmas cards and porcelain, too. As a point of interest, when the Prince and Princess of Wales formally opened the new Alexandra Park in 1882, the Princess was presented with a bouquet of seaweed. According to *The Seaweed Shop*, such bouquets lasted two / three years without attention of any kind!

Arthur Moulton photograph of late-Victorian Old Town fishermen mending nets. Note distinctive boat registration letters "RX" daubed on basket.

A children's book of particular interest to Hastings Old Town is *The Little Weaver* from 1932, on the life of Thomas Hull, 1831 - 1906, Pastor of the Ebenezer Strict and Particular Baptist Chapel in Ebenezer Road. By local author C. Midmer, it has good photographs and a foreword by K. Brooker. Hull is listed in local directories from 1874/75 until 1904 as Pastor, and he edited *The Little Gleaner* and *The Sower* magazines. Arthur Moulton's photographs of Old Hastings were shown, too.

Here I have written about some of the items displayed on 15th October 2008 as I hope they may be of interest to readers - and James Burton's new town of St. Leonards was certainly <u>not</u> overlooked, a bound copy of unusually large engravings being to hand. (Indeed, the subject of St. Leonards is well covered within this book).

I had two happy surprises on that afternoon. Alongside *Sand and Shingle, Jest and Jingle*, featuring the Victorians' love of word-play, I naturally took along a couple of *Punch and Judy* items. After all, where would we (and the seaside) be without rascally Mr. Punch, he being mentioned within Samuel Pepys's Diary of the 1660s. Traditionally Mr. Punch is always accompanied by a "Professor" - his "helpmate". The name of "Professor" Blazier, from All Saints Street, (a predecessor of the legendary "Professor" Percy Press) is mentioned within my father's notes. A gentleman whose wife is a descendant of "Professor" Blazier introduced himself, this providing an interesting link. Secondly, the young man pictured in Boat No. 34 in the middle of the Old Town Boating Lake during the 1950s, (Page 82), was present for my talk and made himself known. On holiday from New Zealand where he now lives, Brian Tubbs, like me, has, with the passage of time, seen many changes.

(See Pages 4, 20, 23, 65, 68, 78, 97, 137 and 193 for other bookish memories, including recollections of local booksellers).

Cynthia Wright (née Scrivens)
2009

◄○►

The Frontispiece of Francis Frith's celebrated book, showing St. Mary-in-the-Castle Church from the beach. Note bathing-machines.

Will we ever know the reason for this highly detailed photograph to the right? Probably not, but a very special occasion has been recorded, judging by the "Sunday best" attire and button-holes - two dahlias, a pink, and a rose - whilst one member of the party eschews such frippery altogether.

An old handwritten card with the picture quotes "Lassie", perhaps the name of the boat, and "Gal Burton, Geo. Dann, Priggy Ball and Tootoo Breeds", four of the Old Towners depicted. Could the unnamed fifth be a "Boy Ashore"? Possibly he in the flat cap. Were they partners in the boat? It seems rather too many, but maybe they had other craft.

(The compiler has taken the above from 1978/79 detail left by her late father who referred to the Nicknames section within his copy of "The Fishing Luggers of Hastings, Parts I and II", by James Hornell, a reprint of Hornell's writings from "The Mariner's Mirror", July and October 1938. At the same time, her father also noted that the name of "Priggy Ball" is quoted within Appendix III of J. M. Baines's "Historic Hastings").

Off All Saints Street (originally Fish or Fisher Street) is Crown Lane, where this slate plaque, unveiled in September 1995, may be found. It was produced by stone-engraver, Michael Renton, whose other projects include restoration work at Winchester Cathedral. The three-storey tenement block **Scrivens Buildings** was erected in 1872/3 but demolished in 1978, with 1980s Crown Court now on the site. The block was constructed of ferro-concrete, very advanced for its time, and formed part of the *Hastings Cottage Improvement Society* with which the Scrivens family was closely connected, one of the three founders in 1857 being a Scrivens. Incorporated in 1861, to this day the initials *H. C. I. S.* are visible on some Old Town properties: see detail on Page 3 for the front cover of this book. **Scrivens Buildings** was intended specifically to house fishing families who needed to be close to The Stade to take advantage of favourable weather conditions at a time when boats were dependent on wind power. **Scrivens Buildings** can be seen within Plate 11.

The date of 1779 refers to the arrival in Hastings, from Dorking, of the first Scrivens, to become landlord of the famous *Swan* coaching inn, High Street. 1871 saw the death of his elder grandson during his fourth Mayoral term, with the last of the four family members commemorated here dying in 1887, all of them, in many different ways, spearheading the town's advancement. (See Page 6).

OLD TOWN FISHERMEN

New look of Hastings

HARRY GOLOMBEK

The Times and Hastings International Chess Congress opens at the Falaise Hall at Hastings in four days' time. There has been one change in the list of entries I gave some weeks ago, Suetin replacing Cholmov as the second Soviet player. So the list now reads as follows:—Stein and Suetin (U.S.S.R.), Gheorghiu (Rumania), Hort (Czechoslovakia), Kaplan (Puerto Rico), Ostojic (Yugoslavia) and from the United Kingdom, Basman, Hartston, Keene and Whiteley.

The addition of the name The Times to the usual Hastings Chess Congress may seem a little unfamiliar at first, though one hopes as the years go by that it will come naturally to the lips of all chess-players; but in fact there was a journalistic connexion between this paper and the Hastings tournaments as long ago as 1895. The first daily reports The Times printed of any tournament were those of the great Hastings Tournament of 1895. The then chess correspondent, Samuel Tinsley, both played in and reported the tournament and presumably The Times also contributed to the sum of £35 which figures in the tournament book as coming from press subscriptions.

The details of the finance of the 1895 tournament are remarkable. Despite a handsome prize fund of £627 10s. which, I suppose, represents in present-day terms some £3,000, they actually made a profit of a little under £20 on the event. There was also substantial help from the town council and entrance fees came to £105, and much too was owed to the hard work put in by the honorary secretary, H. E. Dobell.

The original idea of the tournament was his and Hastings chess owed an enormous amount to the enthusiasm of this gentle, sweet-tempered old man, as he was when I first made his acquaintance on competing in the British Boys Championship at Hastings some 40 years ago. A couple of years later I chanced to be seated next to him at a symphony concert in London and I discovered that his other great passion was for music. In those days there was a Hastings Symphony Orchestra which gave daily concerts at the White Rock Pavilion, just in front of the Falaise Hall, and the chess congress was held on another floor.

One of the pleasures of taking part in the Hastings Congresses was that, when one's game was finished, one could slip out from one floor to another and listen to the music of Mozart and Beethoven instead of watching Alekhine or Capablanca playing. I regret now that I did not question Dobell closely as to the doings and personalities of the great 1895 tournament. Only later was I affected by the cry of: "And did you once see Shelley plain?" When one is young it is the great players of one's own time, in my case Alekhine and Capablanca, who occupy the mind to the exclusion of those of the past. Now, however, I would dearly love to know how such great masters as Pillsbury, Tchigorin, Lasker, Steinitz, Tarrasch and Schlechter behaved during their four-hour session at the Brassey Institute. As it is, apart from the information given in the tournament book and some organizational details, the only light I have been given on the character and habits of these great men is that Tchigorin, on making his first acquaintance with whisky at Hastings, gave it as his considered opinion that it was too weak a drink. From other accounts of his drinking habits one gathers that Tchigorin would have had his own reasons for failing to see Shelley plain.

The hours and rate of play were a little different then from those obtaining nowadays. Instead of a five-hour session from 2 till 7 in the evening with a rate of play of 40 moves in 2½ hours, they had a four-hour session from 1 to 5, adjourned games being resumed from 7 to 10 p.m. and a time limit of 30 moves in two hours, with 15 moves per hour thereafter. As will be observed, rather slower than our present rate. Not that this prevented them from getting into time trouble and losing on time. In fact, in the very first round Tarrasch lost on time to James Mason, just on the thirtieth move. What made this especially irritating for him was that he had a won position and, moreover, was sure he had made 30 moves.

The reason for his mistake is an unusual one: it seems that the doctor had written his name at move one. Mason had done his best to warn his opponent. He drew Tarrasch's attention to his clock more than once and informed him that he had made only 29 moves. Happily this did not affect his position in the prize list. Pillsbury was first with 16½, Tchigorin second with 16, Lasker third with 15½ and Tarrasch fourth with 14. So he would have been fourth with 15 too.

From The Times, 23rd December, 1967.